The Practice of Social Work
with Older Adults

The Practice of Social Work with Older Adults

Insights and Opportunities for a Growing Profession

by

Mary Kaplan, M.S.W., LCSW

Baltimore • London • Sydney

Health Professions Press, Inc.
Post Office Box 10624
Baltimore, Maryland 21285-0624

www.healthpropress.com

Cover and interior designs by Erin Geoghegan.
Typeset by Absolute Service, Inc., Towson, MD.
Manufactured in the United States of America by Versa Press, Inc., East Peoria, IL.

The information provided in this book is in no way meant to substitute for the advice or opinion of a medical, legal, or other professional expert. This book is sold without warranties of any kind, express or implied, and the publisher and authors disclaim any liability, loss, or damage caused by the contents of this book.

The names of the individuals described in this book have been changed to respect their privacy.

Library of Congress Cataloging-in-Publication Data

Names: Kaplan, Mary, author.
Title: The practice of social work with older adults : insights and
    opportunities for a growing profession / by Mary Kaplan, M.S.W., LCSW .
Description: 1 Edition. | Baltimore : Health Professions Press, 2020. |
    Includes bibliographical references and index.
Identifiers: LCCN 2019058047 (print) | LCCN 2019058048 (ebook) | ISBN
    9781938870866 (paperback) | ISBN 9781938870873 (epub)
Subjects: LCSH: Social work with older people—United States. | Older
    people—Services for—United States. | Aging—United States.
Classification: LCC HV1461 .K357 2020 (print) | LCC HV1461 (ebook) | DDC
    362.6/7532—dc23
LC record available at https://lccn.loc.gov/2019058047
LC ebook record available at https://lccn.loc.gov/2019058048

This book is dedicated to my first social work professor,
the late Elizabeth Harvey,
who was an inspiration and source of support
as I took the first steps to what was to become
a challenging and fulfilling social work career.

Contents

About the Author

Mary Kaplan, M.S.W., is a licensed clinical social worker who has worked in health care and geriatrics for over four decades as a clinician, administrator, educator, consultant, and community activist. An instructor since 1971, Kaplan served for 13 years as Director of the Student Internship Program at the University of South Florida School of Aging Studies, where she taught courses on mental health and aging, geriatric care management, and Alzheimer's disease. She earned a bachelor's degree in social work from State University of New York at Buffalo and a master's degree in social work from Catholic University.

Kaplan is the author/coauthor of three books on dementia care (*Behaviors in Dementia, Special Care Programs for Persons with Dementia,* and *Clinical Practice with Caregivers of Dementia Patients*), as well as two additional books on African American history (*Solomon Carter Fuller: Where My Caravan Has Rested* and *The Tuskegee Veterans Hospital and Its Black Physicians*).

The author has conducted workshops and presentations throughout the United States, Europe, Canada, and Australia. Having retired from professional practice, she serves as a mental health volunteer for the American Red Cross.

Acknowledgments

This book is a culmination of four decades of social work practice with older adults and their families, many of whom helped to shape my career and inspired me along my own aging journey.

I want to express my appreciation to the colleagues and friends who were supportive of this endeavor and who generously shared their expertise in reviewing the manuscript and providing valuable suggestions. A special thanks to Stephanie Kastan for her editorial support in the final stages of the book. I am especially grateful for the love and support of my husband, Roy Kaplan, who encouraged me to put these stories on paper in what he sometimes called a "brain dump," as well as the support of my family, especially four of the next generation of writers, my granddaughters.

Introduction

IT WAS JUNE 30, 2015, the last official day of a career in social work that had spanned 41 years. As I closed the door to my empty office and took one last look at the familiar yellow walls, now minus their pictures and plaques, I was overwhelmed by memories of my clients—their expressions of pain, frustration, anger, and yes, even joy when learning how to successfully live with their personal struggles. That room had borne witness to some amazing stories.

The decision to become a social worker was not one that I made early in life. For many women graduating from high school in the 1960s, career choices were limited, and most became secretaries, teachers, or nurses. My passion was fashion, so after graduation from high school, I entered the Fashion Institute of Technology. I worked as a bridal consultant until I got married and moved to Maine, where my husband began his graduate studies. Located in Orono, a small town outside of Bangor, the University of Maine was situated in a wooded area, with the smell of the local pulp mill permeating the air. The opportunities for employment were limited, particularly in the fashion industry, so I took a job at the university bookstore. By this time, I was reconsidering my original plan to pursue a career in the fashion industry. The war in Vietnam and the rural poverty that I saw in Maine made me realize that fashion was not high on the list of societal priorities.

When a position as an interviewer for a research project became available at the university, I made the life-changing decision to apply for the job. The project was designed to evaluate maternal healthcare services available to low-income women living on the small islands near the town of Bar Harbor. My job was to travel to these islands, some only accessible by small ferries, and interview women who had given birth within the past 2 years. As I knocked on torn screen doors; sat in sparsely furnished homes; and talked to the wives of lobster fishermen, worm farmers, and laborers, I began to develop confidence in my ability to listen with empathy and to understand their needs and concerns.

Although the spark had been ignited, it would be another 2 years before I would be able to take the necessary steps toward becoming a social worker. It was 1972 when I entered the bachelor of social work (B.S.W.) program at SUNY at Buffalo (now commonly referred to as the University at Buffalo), where my husband had taken a faculty position in the sociology department. At the end of my first year, the time had come to arrange an internship. While most of my classmates were requesting placements in mental health settings or children's services, I made the decision to work with older adults. My experiences with older family members, friends, and neighbors over the years had led me to develop an interest in this population. My parents, who were both healthcare professionals, had also exposed me to healthcare settings, where I had frequently observed the neglect and poor treatment of older adults.

This was a time before the social work profession had begun to significantly address the needs of older adults. With few exceptions, most social work education programs offered no courses on geriatric social work, and students were not encouraged to pursue a career in this field. Although the School of Social Work at SUNY at Buffalo did not offer any courses on aging, there was one faculty member who had an interest in older adults, and he arranged an internship for me in a nursing home. I was the only student in my B.S.W. class who expressed an interest in working with older adults, and I found the negative reactions of my fellow classmates disappointing. It was an attitude that I would encounter throughout much of my career in geriatric social work.

My internship site, the Episcopal Church Home for the Elderly, was a nonprofit home operated by the Episcopal Diocese of Buffalo, located on the city's west side. The home's resident population was mostly female and ranged in age from 66 to 97, with most residents in their 80s. Although it was still the custom for most older frail and ill adults to be cared for by their families at this time, the nursing home was often the only option for those without family support. Alternative levels of care for older adults, such as assisted living and specialized care programs, did not exist. The Episcopal Church Home was originally intended to be a home for older adults without illnesses or disabilities. Requirements for admission included being ambulatory and in fairly good health.

But, as the residents aged, many developed dementia, incontinence, and the inability to walk without assistance. To meet residents' increasing needs, the Episcopal Church Home built an adjoining nursing facility that could provide a higher level of care.

Considering that there were few men in the social work profession and even fewer working with older adults, I was surprised to find that my internship preceptor was male. I could not have chosen a better teacher or role model. My preceptor's genuine concern and respect for the residents made a lasting impression on me. My internship at the Episcopal Church Home not only provided me with a greater understanding of older adults and valuable social work skills, but also strengthened my desire to work with this population. Many of us enter the social work profession with the goal of "saving the world." Though a lofty goal, it is one that can easily lead to personal and professional burnout. As I soon learned, however, satisfaction can be found in improving the life of just one person. Below is a story from my first year at the Episcopal Church Home. Throughout this book, personal stories and experiences from my career are presented as shown here.

A new admission to the Episcopal Church Home, Margaret had been moved from her home in another state to Buffalo by her son. He had promised his mother that her stay there was only temporary and that he would eventually be moving her into his home to live with his family. After several weeks went by, there were fewer and fewer visits by her son, who kept postponing his mother's move to his home. Margaret soon realized that her son never intended to keep his promise and that his plan was for her to remain at the nursing home. Feeling depressed and hopeless, Margaret began refusing to get out of bed, get dressed, or eat.

Determined to brighten Margaret's mood and facilitate her adjustment to her new residence, I thought that taking her out for an afternoon would give her some pleasure. The idea was not welcomed by the nursing staff, as this was outside of the norm and they considered it a lot of unnecessary trouble, but I persuaded them to get Margaret dressed and help her into my car. As we drove away, I asked Margaret where she wanted to go. She replied, "Take me to the water." So off we went, heading for the park at Lake Erie.

On the way, Margaret asked if we could stop to pick up a soda and a pack of cigarettes, pleasures that she had been denied at the nursing home. For about an hour, the two of us sat in the car on the water's edge, enjoying one of Buffalo's rare sunny afternoons. Margaret spoke very little as she looked out at the lake, sipping her soda and taking puffs from her cigarette.

Later, when we returned to the nursing home, Margaret didn't want to budge from the car and end our afternoon. It was a struggle to get her back inside that building, even with the assistance of nursing staff. Two weeks later, Margaret died. Still, I took solace that she had enjoyed some of life's simple pleasures and a taste of freedom shortly before she passed.

My desire to improve life for people like Margaret helped solidify my resolve to embark on a career in geriatric social work. Following graduation, I accepted a casework position at the Erie County Office for the Aging. Several years later, when searching for a social work graduate program, I found that little had changed when it came to programs that offered courses in geriatric social work. The year was 1977, and the social work profession still had not embraced the geriatric client population. Although it did not offer courses in geriatric social work, I chose to attend Catholic University in Washington, D.C. to obtain my master of social work (M.S.W.) degree. The incentive of a scholarship and an advanced M.S.W. program for B.S.W. graduates (which meant that I could complete my degree in 12 months) ultimately convinced me that this school would be a good choice for my graduate studies.

Although I was unable to take courses on aging, I did have the opportunity to complete an internship at the Fairfax County Area Agency on Aging, located in Fairfax, Virginia, where, as the agency's first intern, I participated in the development of several programs for older adults. During my internship, I also had the opportunity to produce a consumers' guide to housing alternatives in northern Virginia and to develop and conduct a research project that became the basis for my master's thesis, *A Needs Assessment of the Elderly by Community Agencies and Organizations*.

Several months after my retirement from social work, I received an invitation to give a guest lecture at the University at Buffalo (UB), where I had earned my bachelor's degree in social work in 1974. The UB School of Social Work had made a commitment to train social work students to work with older adults and thought that, in sharing my experiences in the field of aging and healthcare, I could provide some insight into the many job opportunities that existed in this field.

To announce a retirement is on some level a way of stage-managing one's own legacy. As I prepared my lecture, I realized what a diverse and wonderful social work career I had enjoyed and the changes that had taken place in the profession of social work over the preceding 41 years. Many memories, long forgotten, surfaced during those 4 days that I spent in Buffalo. As I walked into the classroom to give my first lecture to the small group of graduate students who were planning to work with older adults, I realized that this was the same building where I had taken my first social work classes over 43 years ago.

For the next 3 days, I had the opportunity to talk to the faculty, students, and social workers from Buffalo's community aging services and programs. In addition to my presentation to the M.S.W. students, I also gave a lecture to an undergraduate class, taped an interview with a faculty member for future use in the classroom, and met with advanced students in the UB School of Social Work's Hartford Partnership Program for Aging Education. Driving through the city brought back additional memories of the clients whose lives I had been inspired to improve with my newly learned social work skills, people who had taught me lessons that I would remember throughout my career. I started to write some of these stories down, and the idea for this book was born.

My purpose for writing this book was to create an awareness of the rewards and challenges of working with the geriatric population and the opportunities that exist for social workers to improve the quality of life for older adults. The book is written for social work students who are making decisions about a practice specialty, as well as social workers who are considering a move to geriatric practice or are now working with clients who are aging or caring for older family members. This book is also a salute to and a resource for other social workers who are proud to call themselves "geriatric social workers."

About this Book

The chapters that follow provide a brief history of the social work profession and the development of geriatric social work (Section I); principles for professional work with older adults (Section II); issues faced by older adults, about which the social worker must be knowledgeable to engage in a successful and ethical practice (Section III); and settings and opportunities for geriatric social work (Section IV).

Following are some terms used commonly throughout the book:

- *Aging*: the lifelong process of growing older.

- *Alzheimer's disease*: a degenerative disease that attacks the brain and results in impaired memory, thinking, and behavior. Alzheimer's disease is the most common cause of dementia.

- *Average life expectancy*: the age at which 50 percent of the members of a population have died, when plotted on a standard survival curve. This statistic is normally calculated from birth but may be recomputed in terms of expected years remaining at any age.

- *Dementia*: a syndrome characterized by a decline in intellectual functioning. Dementia may be caused by more than 70 diseases, the most common being Alzheimer's disease.

- *Demography*: the study of a population and those variables bringing about changes in that population. Variables studied by demographers are age, sex, race, education, income, geographic trends, birth, and death.

- *Generation*: often used as a synonym for cohort, the term is also applied within the context of the family (e.g., children form one generation, their parents another, their grandparents a third).

- *Geriatrics*: the branch of medicine specializing in the healthcare and treatment of older adults. It is defined by the World Health Organization as the branch of medicine that is concerned with the health of older adults in all aspects: preventive, clinical, remedial, rehabilitative, and continuous monitoring.

- *Gerontology*: the multidisciplinary study of all aspects of aging, including health-related, biological, sociological, economic, behavioral, and environmental.

- *Lifespan*: the maximum lifespan of a population is the characteristic observed age of death for its very oldest individual(s). Average lifespan is the age at which 50 percent of the members of a population have died.

- *Longevity*: the condition or quality of being long-lived.

- *Medicare*: a federal entitlement program of medical insurance for persons aged 65 and over or with disabilities that is provided through the Social Security system.

- *Retirement*: the period or life stage following termination of and withdrawal from a regular job and from income from employment. Retirement is often difficult to determine because some older persons retire from one job and take another full- or part-time job.

- *Social Security*: a national insurance program that provides income to workers when they retire or if they have disabilities and to dependent survivors when a worker dies. Retirement payments are based on workers' earnings during employment.

The successes and challenges encountered in the practice of geriatric social work are illustrated using practice experiences and real-life client stories. Identifying information about clients has been changed to protect confidentiality.

The Development of Geriatric Social Work

Section I describes the origins of social work in the United States and follows its development as a profession. Social work has been influenced by the changes in our country and the issues faced by its citizens. The growth of the older population, the recognition of the needs and issues facing older adults, and the response by the social work profession to meeting those needs are discussed.

CHAPTER 1

The Evolution of the Social Work Profession and Geriatric Social Work

KEY POINTS

- Many sociocultural changes have affected the growth of the social work profession in the United States.

- The National Association of Social Workers (NASW) and the Council on Social Work Education (CSWE) have played major roles in establishing professional standards and guidelines for the practice of social work.

- The growth of the country's older population has led to the development of geriatric social work as a practice specialty.

BY THE TIME I BEGAN my social work career in 1974, the social work profession had experienced many changes and tremendous growth. Social work practice and education have always been influenced by the changing world in which we live. The growth of the social work profession coincided with those periods of our country's history that witnessed increasing government intervention to address economic issues related to poverty, unemployment, workplace conditions, and the political rights of workers. Along with the growing involvement of social work in societal welfare, social workers played an increasingly important role in another movement in the United States, the mental hygiene movement. A focus on the treatment of mental health conditions led to the development of social psychiatry, in which a patient is regarded not only as an individual, but also as a social unit.

As in most professions, the quest for status and identity within the field of social work has been ongoing. The profession acquired much of its political power and status through its association with both reform activities and the creation of services in the public and private sectors. Much of this took place during the Progressive Era (1890–1917); the New Deal period (1933–1940); and the 1960s and 1970s, which marked the era of President Johnson's social programs, the War on Poverty, and grassroots community organizing. However, the earliest origins of social work as a profession can be traced back even further.

History of the Social Work Profession in the United States

The origins of social work have been attributed to the settlement movement, which took place over a century ago. The settlement movement, which originated in England in 1884 with the founding of Toynbee Hall, began in the United States in 1886 with the opening of the first settlement house in New York. Jane Addams, considered to be a social work pioneer, opened the famous Hull House in Chicago 3 years later. The settlement movement grew in response to the employment problems faced by immigrants and low-income residents of America's growing urban centers. Its birth was the result of economic factors in society that led to hardships for the working class, especially immigrants.

Another issue of importance for early social workers was the treatment of people with mental illnesses. The very first meeting of the National Conference of Social Work (then known as the Conference of Boards of Public Charities), held in 1874, was primarily focused on insanity and its treatment.[1] This growing awareness of the need for reform and education in the field of nervous and mental diseases resulted in the formation of the National Committee for Mental Hygiene, with several social work leaders as charter members.[2] The establishment of psychopathic hospitals was one of the most significant examples of changes in the treatment of persons with mental illnesses that were brought about by the mental hygiene movement. These hospitals were designed to admit patients of all socioeconomic levels for examination, observation, and short-term intensive mental health treatment. Their outpatient departments provided free consultation and home care to people living in poverty.

From this existing model of medical social work, it was only a small step to the development of psychiatric social work, beginning in

Massachusetts in 1912. Not long afterward, William Sulzer, the governor of New York, authorized state hospital superintendents to establish outpatient departments to facilitate the readjustment of patients following psychiatric hospitalization. The important role of the social worker in the treatment of mental illnesses was now recognized, as social work was charged with facilitating the discharge and aftercare of patients, as well as investigating their history, habits, home and working conditions, and other causes of mental illness to apply corrective and preventive measures.

The question of whether social work could be classified as a profession was raised as far back as 1915 in the proceedings of the National Conference of Charities and Correction.[3] The return of World War I veterans led to new challenges and opportunities for the social work field, prompting the rise of psychiatric social work as a profession. The close collaboration between psychiatry and social work during this period could be seen in the efforts of Dr. Elmer E. Southard and social worker Mary C. Jarrett at the Boston Psychopathic Hospital. The two helped to develop a program offered by Smith College that trained social workers to work with soldiers returning from the war with "shell shock" and other traumatic mental disorders.[4] The problem of rehabilitating these veterans dramatized, as few other problems had, the need for integrating psychiatric techniques with social work.

During this same time period, mental health and social work became integrated in other areas as well. In the years following World War I, there were also advances in the application of mental hygiene to the study and treatment of behavior problems in children. The child guidance movement began in 1922 with the establishment of mental hygiene clinics in connection with children's courts and in institutions for children displaying juvenile delinquency.

The 1920s also saw the development of the field of personnel relations in industry. It was thought that teams composed of psychiatrists, psychologists, and social workers could be invaluable in selecting personnel on a scientific basis by matching personal characteristics and relational style to job criteria. These professionals could also help to treat the emotional problems of individual workers as well as general problems of personnel relations to the mutual benefit of employee and employer. This concept, the basis for today's employee assistance programs (EAPs), was not readily accepted by employers or employees. It was not until the 1940s, with the development of occupational alcohol programs that addressed the negative impact of alcohol abuse on workplace productivity and performance, that organizations started to offer EAP services to employees. The focus of these programs expanded as organizations recognized that alcohol was not the only issue affecting employees in the workplace. With the growth of EAPs, legislation was passed in the 1970s that institutionalized them in federal agencies. At this time, private EAPs were established to offer services via contracts to employers. Four models developed: internal, external, hybrid, and consortium. The expansion of EAPs eventually included services to employees' family members.[5]

From the 1930s through the 1960s, the development of the U.S. welfare state led to a focus on the labor market within the social work profession, particularly its economic, social, and psychological effects. During the Great Depression, social workers joined with other activists to advocate for emergency relief measures, unemployment insurance, and the old-age provisions of the Social Security Act. Social work incorporated an understanding of both the socioeconomic and psychosocial dimensions of work into its conceptual framework. This insight distinguished social work from other mental health professions that, with few exceptions, ignored the impact of issues such as workplace pressures, economic insecurity, and unemployment on individuals.

The Definition of Social Work

In 1956, a working definition of social work practice was created by the newly formed National Association of Social Workers (NASW) with the understanding that it would be revised continuously as knowledge of client needs and the methods of practice best suited to meet those needs grew. In 1959, the Council on Social Work Education (CSWE) published the results of a study on social work curricula and reported that there was "a lack of a single, widely recognized, or generally accepted statement of the aims and purposes of social work."[6] CSWE recognized the need for social work education programs to share a common commitment to educate qualified, ethical social work professionals and developed standards for the accreditation of baccalaureate programs, which were implemented in 1974.

With roots in social casework, the practice of clinical social work demonstrated a shift in focus from people and their social environment to individuals, families, and groups. In addition to practicing clinical social work in agency settings, social workers increasingly moved into independent private practice. This trend led the NASW to acknowledge private practice as a setting for the delivery of clinical social work services. In 1961, the NASW Board of Directors approved a definition of private practitioners of social work:

> Private practitioners are social workers who, wholly or in part, practice social work outside a governmental or duly incorporated voluntary agency, who have responsibility for their own practice and set up conditions of exchange with their clients, and who identify themselves as social work practitioners in offering services.[7]

The NASW published its first *Handbook on the Private Practice of Social Work* in 1967. Clinical social work was formally recognized by NASW in 1978 as a practice specialty that requires a specific set of knowledge and skills. A task force on clinical social work was established at this time, which became the Provisional Council of Clinical Social Work in 1982. The council developed this definition of clinical social work, which was approved by the NASW Board of Directors in January of 1984:

> Clinical social work shares with all social work practice the goal of enhancement and maintenance of psychosocial functioning of individuals, families, and small groups. Clinical social work practice is the professional application of social work theory and methods to the treatment and prevention of psychosocial dysfunction, disability, or impairment, including emotional and mental disorders. It is based on knowledge of one or more theories of human development within a psychosocial context. The perspective of person-in-situation is central to clinical social work practice. Clinical social work includes interventions directed to interpersonal interactions, intrapsychic dynamics, and life-support and management issues. Clinical social work services consist of assessment; diagnosis; treatment, including psychotherapy and counseling; client-centered advocacy; consultation; and evaluation. The process of clinical social work is undertaken within the objectives of social work and the principles and values contained in the NASW Code of Ethics.[7]

The Development of Geriatric Social Work

In 2006, the U.S. Department of Health and Human Services (HHS) released a report to Congress, *The Supply and Demand of Professional Social Workers Providing Long-term Care Services*. This report was the first government analysis in recent history of the anticipated demand for geriatric social workers resulting from the rapid growth of the older population. As the baby boomer generation hits retirement age, the number of individuals aged 65 and older is expected to increase from 35 million in the year 2000 to over 86 million by 2050, with older adults comprising nearly 21% of the population.

The growth of the older population has been attributed to two converging trends: increasing life expectancy and decreasing birthrates. Life expectancy at birth rose in the United States from 47.3 years in 1900 to 78.69 years in 2016.[8] When coupled with decreasing birthrates, changes in life expectancy have significantly increased the number of older adults and their proportion of the total population. Contributing to an increase in lifespan has been the dramatic reduction of mortality earlier in life. Better treatment of infectious diseases and complications of childbirth has made it possible for higher percentages of the population to survive until old age.

With age as a strong predictor of the need for both acute and long-term care services (i.e., skilled nursing care, alternative residential care, and home- and community-based care), it was anticipated that the number of persons requiring these services could grow to 19 million by 2050.[9] This trend increases the demand for professional social workers because they provide critical services such as care coordination, case management, mental health services and supports, determination of eligibility for government programs, caregiver support, and counseling.

The HHS study concluded that the need for social workers to serve this population was much greater than the supply, suggesting three major barriers to attracting social work students to the aging field: (1) limited numbers of adequately trained faculty to influence students to choose field placements in aging programs or long-term care settings, (2) a lack of institutional supports for geriatric curricula, and (3) the absence of financial supports and incentives for students in training.[9,10]

Lack of Emphasis on Geriatric Studies in Educational Programs

Although the growing demand for geriatric social workers is evident, educational training in this field is limited. The majority of B.S.W. and M.S.W. programs still contain little or no gerontological content.

According to the CSWE in 2000, only 3% of master's degree students were enrolled in aging or gerontology programs, and 80% of B.S.W. students graduated without taking a single course in aging.[11] Many social workers have been reluctant to work with this population and have not pursued aging as a field of study.

In 1994, CSWE reported that only 2.1% of M.S.W. students in the United States indicated a primary interest in aging. This figure was less than half of what was reported in 1990. A national study of licensed social workers, conducted by NASW and the Center for Health Workforce Studies at SUNY Albany in 2006, found an equally alarming trend—the number of new social workers providing services to older adults had decreased.[12] In the same year, data from the Bureau of Labor Statistics indicated that only 28% of social workers had focused on caring for older adults.[13]

To give an idea of the pressing need for geriatric social workers, Florida's population has the highest proportion of older adults and ranks third among all states in terms of the total number of older residents, yet studies in geriatric social work have not been prominently featured in Florida colleges and universities, a fact that I can attest to by experience. As the only faculty member in the University of South Florida's School of Aging Studies with a social work degree, I often received requests to give guest lectures on aging to the school's B.S.W. students. This lecture was usually presented during the last week of their human development course. In the 13 years that I was on the faculty, from 1997 to 2010, the social work program at the University of South Florida offered no aging courses or field placement sites where students could work with older adults. Students who expressed an interest in the aging field were often discouraged by social work faculty. Concerned about meeting the increased demand for skilled, knowledgeable professionals to help care for the growing older population, NASW's Florida Chapter created a committee on aging in 1995. Committee members—social workers from both academic and community settings—focused their efforts on increasing the number of continuing education opportunities in geriatric social work within the state of Florida. These efforts included adding sessions on older adults to professional state and local conference programs and having committee members serve as speakers at these events.

The United States is not the only country tasked with training a skilled workforce to care for its growing older population. Population aging has been occurring in every country in the world. Currently, 8.5% of the world's population is 65 and older. By 2050, this percentage is projected to grow to nearly 17% of the world's population.[14] Countries with high percentages of citizens who are 65 years and older include Japan (26.3%), Italy (22.4%), Greece (21.4%), and Germany (21.2%).[15] Major contributing factors to the growth of the older population worldwide have been diminishing fertility rates and longer lifespans. To adapt to the growth of aging populations, many countries have raised the retirement age, reduced pension benefits, and increased spending on care for older adults.

Australia is an example of another country that has been working to address the anticipated demand for geriatric social workers and other skilled professionals involved in the care of older adults. With the projected increase in Australia's 65-and-older population from 9% in 1977 to an expected 22% by 2057, the country is anticipating the need for a more skilled labor force and the expansion of education and training programs in aged care.[16] In response, Australia has taken some initial strides to improve education and training for geriatric care workers. In 2004, I traveled to Melbourne, Australia to serve as keynote speaker at The Aged Care Worker Competencies: Opportunities and Threats Conference, where I addressed the process of implementing compulsory education for geriatric care workers in the United States and the outcomes for the geriatric care industry, educators, and staff. During this time, Melbourne's aging network was in the process of creating workplace policies and instituting government regulations that would affect geriatric care workers. Faced with a growing older population and a significant number of older adults who had been identified as having cognitive impairments, Victoria University had also developed a multidisciplinary graduate program in aged services, the only one in Australia. There are currently 13 educational institutions in Australia offering courses on the care of older adults.

Lack of Financial Support and Incentives for Geriatric Social Workers

Additional reasons for the lack of interest in geriatric social work are lower compensation and fewer financial incentives. Salary is a major disincentive to pursuing geriatric social work. In 1999, the annual income for full-time social workers was lowest for those employed in nursing facilities and hospices. Similar findings were noted in 2002.[17,18] According to the Bureau of Labor Statistics in 2017, the annual salary for a geriatric social worker ranged from $19,500 to $113,000 nationally, with lower salaries reported for social workers employed in nursing facilities.[19]

As a way to increase the number of qualified professionals in the field of geriatrics, workforce incentives are often put in place. One such incentive is student loan forgiveness in exchange for service, a program that is often a combination of public and private efforts to attract professionals to work in underserved areas such as the care of older adults. For example, in the United States, the National Health Service Corps offers loan forgiveness programs to physicians, nurse practitioners, midwives, and other healthcare professionals in exchange for a 2-year commitment to work in underserved areas. Similar programs exist for lawyers, physicians, Peace Corps volunteers, and teachers who agree to work in public service positions in low-income communities.

At the federal and state levels, loan forgiveness programs for social workers have given awards for specialization and service in underserved populations such as high-risk, low-income children and families, but not for service with older adults. One exception is New York, which funds a Licensed Social Worker Loan Forgiveness Program through the New York State Higher Education Services Corporation. This program funds loan repayments for social work graduates who are employed in shortage areas that include aging, health, mental health, child welfare, and HIV/AIDS.[20]

Better training and incentive programs are one way of attracting more people to geriatric social work, but another important issue is also at stake. Based on my personal experiences working with social work students and colleagues, I believe that few in the profession choose to specialize in this area because of the low value placed on our aging population for many years. Those of us who do choose to work with older adults can experience low professional prestige. This issue is not exclusive to social work but is also seen in other healthcare and social service professions, such as medicine and nursing.

Education and Employment in Geriatric Social Work: Current and Future Opportunities

Social workers who serve older adults have the opportunity to work in a variety of settings. Some examples of practice settings include inpatient and outpatient psychiatric services, acute care hospitals, nursing homes, home health agencies, hospice programs, adult day care, senior centers, and Area Agencies on Aging and their related Older Americans Act programs. The growth of care management services for older adults has led to new opportunities for social workers in private practice and managed care settings. Even those social workers who work primarily with children, youth, and families will spend significant time in their careers dealing with issues that involve older adults, such as grandparents raising grandchildren, multigenerational households, and family caregiving. It is estimated that more than 75% of social workers end up working with older adults and their families in some capacity even though they never intended to do so.[21]

Although the social work profession has been slow to keep pace with the growing needs of older adults, the past few years have seen increased support of social workers in the field of aging on the part of NASW through continuing education offerings, professional standards for social work practice, NASW publications, government-relations activities, a specialty practice section, and a professional credential in aging. The Geriatric Social Work Initiative, supported by the John A. Hartford Foundation, is collaborating with social work education programs to train faculty to conduct research and teach, mentor, and prepare social work students to serve older adults. The Hartford Foundation has also established the Hartford Doctoral Fellows Program in Geriatric Social Work to recruit, support, and prepare doctoral students to work with older adults; as well as their Practicum Partnership Program, which develops models for aging-focused field education at schools of social work and community agencies. Their National Center for Gerontological Social Work Education promotes changes in curricula and social work programs and develops policy initiatives for the adoption of gerontological educational resources. Another private foundation, The Atlantic Philanthropies, provides funding to create the Institute for Geriatric Social Work (IGSW) at the Boston University School of Social Work. The IGSW was established to improve the quality and effectiveness of training for practicing social workers nationwide and to promote policy initiatives on behalf of the profession.[13]

A federal program that trains the healthcare workforce to serve older adults and family caregivers is the Geriatrics Workforce Enhancement Program (GWEP). Training provided by GWEP sites is available to social work practitioners and students. The program is funded by congressional legislation, which has also attempted to reestablish the Geriatrics Academic Career Award (GACA) Program, a previously funded program for developing academic clinical educators who specialize in aging. Professionals eligible for GACA include social workers.[22]

Another effort to expand the intersection of social work and gerontology is taking place in the academic setting. Beginning in the 1970s, when the University of Southern California started a program in which students could receive a dual master's degree in both social work and gerontology, the concept of a dual degree program has spread to other campuses. One example of a successful program is offered at Wayne State University School of Social Work in Detroit, Michigan. The school's Ph.D. program in social work with a dual degree in gerontology allows social work faculty and researchers trained in geriatrics to promote evidence-based practice and to serve as role models for students specializing in the field.

Although efforts are being made to develop social work initiatives in aging, social work practice with older adults continues to be a stigmatized field of practice because of persisting negative stereotypes about older adults and the view that jobs in the field are not challenging and are poorly paid. To promote the role of social work in geriatric care and to create a workforce of social workers who are trained to work with the growing number of older adults, the profession must not only educate social work faculty and students about aging, but also educate other healthcare professionals, policymakers, employers, payers, and consumers about the value of social work services for older adults and their families.

CHAPTER NOTES

1. Chapin, J. B. (1874). The duty of the states toward their insane poor. *Proceedings of the Conference of Boards of Public Charities, 1,* 5–7.
2. Deutsch, A. (1944). History of mental hygiene. In The American Psychiatric Association (Ed.), *One hundred years of American psychiatry* (pp. 356–358). New York: Columbia University Press.
3. Flexner, A. (1915). Is social work a profession? *Proceedings of the National Conference of Charities and Correction, 42,* 576–590.
4. The New York Times (1918, June 16). Preparing to care for shell-shocked men: Smith College will have a school this summer to train women as assistants to psychiatrists in vitally important work—what Canada has done. *The New York Times,* p. T62.
5. For further reading on EAPs, see Rothermel S, Slavit W, Finch RA, et al. (December 2008). Center for Prevention and Health Services. *An Employer's Guide to Employee Assistance Programs: Recommendations for Strategically Defining, Integrating and Measuring Employee Assistance Programs.* Washington, DC: National Business Group on Health; Attridge, M. (2005). The business case for the integration of employee

assistance, work-life and wellness services: A literature review. *Journal of Work-place Behavioral Health, 20*(1), 31–55; Csiernik, R. (2005). What we are doing in the employee assistance program: Meeting the challenge of the integrated model of practice. *Journal of Workplace Behavioral Health, 21,* 11–22; Herlihy, P.A., & Attridge, M. (2005). Research on the integration of employee assistance, work-life and wellness services: Past, present and future. *Journal of Workplace Behavioral Health, 20*(1–2), 67–93; Haaz, E.J., Maynard, J., Petrica, S.C., & Williams, C.E. (2003). Employee assistance program accreditation: History and outlook. *Employee Assistance Quarterly, 19* (1), 1–26; Maiden, R.P. (2003). Certification, licensure, and accreditation in employee assistance programs. *Employee Assistance Quarterly, 19* (1), 1; Masi, D.A., & Jacobson, J.M. (2003). Outcome measurements of an integrated employee assistance and work-life program. *Research on Social Work Practice, 13*(4), 451–467; Cunningham, G. (1994). *Effective employee assistance programs: A guide for EAP counselors and managers.* Thousand Oaks, CA: SAGE Publications, Inc.

6. Boehm, W.W. (1959). Objectives of the social work curriculum of the future. In Council on Social Work Education. (Ed.), *Social work curriculum study* (Vol. 1), 40. New York: Council on Social Work Education.

7. National Association of Social Workers. (1989). *National standards for the practice of clinical social work.* Washington, DC: National Association of Social Workers.

8. United Nations, Department of Economic and Social Affairs, Population Division. (2017). *World population prospects: The 2017 revision.* New York: United Nations.

9. U.S. Department of Health and Human Services Office of the Assistant Secretary for Planning and Evaluation. (2006). *The supply and demand of professional social workers providing long-term care services: Report to Congress.* Washington, DC: U.S. Department of Health and Human Services.

10. Council on Social Work Education/SAGE-SW. (2001). *Strengthening the impact of social work to improve the quality of life for older adults and their families: A blueprint for the new millennium.* Alexandria, VA: Council on Social Work Education.

11. Galambos, C., & Greene, R.R. (2006). A competency approach to curriculum building: A social work mission. *Journal of Gerontological Social Work, 48*(1–2), 111–126.

12. Whitaker, T., Weismiller, T., Clark, E., & Wilson, M. (2006). *Assuring the sufficiency of a frontline workforce: A national study of licensed social workers. Special report: Social work services in health care settings.* Washington, DC: National Association of Social Workers. Retrieved from https://www.socialworkers.org/LinkClick.aspx?fileticket =OilZ7p_EEnE%3D&portalid=0

13. Institute for Geriatric Social Work (IGSW) and the New York Academy of Medicine (NYAM). (2005, Winter). The shortage of social workers caring for elders and their families. *Social Work, Aging and Public Policy: Bulletin from IGSW and NYAM, 1*(1). Retrieved from https://www.cswe.org/getattachment/Centers-Initiatives/Centers /Gero-Ed-Center/Initiatives/Workforce-Development/Reports-and-Facts-Sheets /IGSW-PolicyBulletinNYAM4-04-05.pdf.aspx

14. He, W., Goodkind, D., & Kowal, P. (2016). *An aging world: 2015* (U.S. Census Bureau, International Population Reports, P95/16-1). Washington, DC: U.S. Government Publishing Office.

15. World Health Organization. (2015). *World report on ageing and health.* Geneva, Switzerland: World Health Organization.

16. Australian Bureau of Statistics (ABS). (2014). *Australian historical population statistics, 2014* (ABS cat. no. 3105.0.65.001). Canberra: ABS.

17. National Association of Social Workers. (2002). Practice research network: Social work income. *PRN, 2:1* (6).

18. The John A. Hartford Foundation. (2009) *Escalating need for geriatric social workers.* Retrieved from https://www.johnahartford.org/ar2009/Escalating_Need_for _Geriatric_Social_Workers.html

19. U.S. Bureau of Labor Statistics. (2018) *Occupational Employment Statistics.* Washington, DC: United States Department of Labor. Retrieved from https:// www.bls.gov/oes/current/oes211029.htm

20. Social Work Leadership Institute (SWLI), New York Academy of Medicine. (2007). *Redefining long-term care: A clear role for social workers in care coordination for older adults.* New York: SWLI.

21. Pace, P. R. (2014, February). Need for geriatric social work grows. *NASW News, 7.* Retrieved from http://www.socialworkblog.org/nasw-news-article/2014/02/need -for-geriatric-social-work-grows/

22. Coleman, M., Dietsche, S., Dorn, C., Herman, C., & Meruvia, R. (2019). *Advocating for social workers in aging, behavioral health, child welfare, clinical social work, health care, school social work.* Washington, DC: The National Association of Social Workers (NASW). Retrieved from https://www.socialworkers.org/LinkClick.aspx ?fileticket=WTauVOClzd0%3d&portalid=0.

Basic Principles of Working with Older Adults

This section introduces social workers to the aging person and the aging process. The chapters that follow present strategies and approaches to treatment that are effective for older adults and address the diversity of this population. Chapter 2 discusses society's often negative stereotypes and misperceptions of older adults. In order to dispel these misperceptions and to provide an accurate picture of aging persons and the aging process, the diverse physical, psychological, and social characteristics of older adults are examined, as well as the influence of culture and history on aging. The increased life expectancy of older adults with intellectual and physical disabilities and its impact on families and community services are also discussed. Chapter 3 emphasizes the need for social workers to develop a sense of their own self-concept that will enable them to understand and help older clients. Basic social work skills that include communication, assessment, and problem-solving are discussed, with suggestions for modifications that are effective in working with older adults. Chapter 4 addresses the ethical issues that social workers encounter when providing care and services to older adults, with an emphasis on the older adult's need for privacy, self-determination, and independence. Chapter 5 provides social workers with a variety of practice strategies and techniques that consider the diversity of this age group. Several therapy models are presented.

CHAPTER 2

Characteristics of Older Adults

KEY POINTS

- Stereotypes of older adults do not consider the diversity of the aging experience.

- Differences in the aging process are related to differences in functional capacity and health status. Limitations, illness, and disability become more common in advanced age (over age 80).

- How people age and how they are treated are influenced by a broad array of factors.

WHEN TEACHING STUDENTS IN MY Introduction to Gerontology course, I would ask them to list the characteristics of older adults on the first day of class. The top three responses I received were that older adults were frail and dependent, had significant memory loss, and were resistant to change. In the social work profession, these stereotypes and variations thereof affect how we interact professionally with older people as well as what our expectations are for success in intervention and treatment (see Table 2.1). Misperceptions and generalizations about older adults have led healthcare and social service professionals to "write them off" as being unresponsive to treatment.

The common stereotypes of older adults come from outdated and selective perceptions that are often based on the false assumption that this is a homogeneous segment of our population—that we all become alike when we turn 65. This arbitrary age used to designate old age was

Table 2.1 Aging: Stereotype vs. Fact

STEREOTYPE	FACT
Most older adults are alike.	They are a very diverse age group.
Older adults are alone and lonely.	Most maintain close contact with family and friends.
Older adults are sick, frail, and dependent on others.	Most older people live independently.
Older people are often cognitively impaired.	Many older adults maintain a high level of cognitive functioning well into their later years. For those who experience decline in some areas of cognitive functioning, it is usually not severe enough to cause problems in daily life.
Older adults are depressed.	Community-dwelling older adults have low rates of depression compared to younger adults.
Older people become more difficult and rigid with age.	Personality remains relatively consistent throughout the lifespan.
Older adults do not cope well with the declines associated with aging.	Most older adults adjust to the challenges of aging.

established in the United States by political agreement and created primarily to define the retirement stage and eligibility for social security benefits. These designations have little or nothing to do with the realities or the relativity of the aging process, nor do they specify a state of physical decline or functional characteristics that apply to all persons aged 65 and older.

In a larger sense, a negative view of old age is more often seen in Western civilization than in Eastern cultures. For example, the Western concept of the life cycle is different from that of Asian cultures. Eastern philosophy places the individual's self, life, and death within the process of the human experience. Life and death are familiar and equally acceptable parts of the meaning of self. Death is characteristically seen as a welcome relief from suffering and, as in Japanese ancestor worship, a step upward in social mobility to join the revered ancestors. In Buddhism, death is merely a passage to another incarnation unless the person achieves an enlightenment that releases him or her from the eternal cycle.[1] In contrast, the cultural views of the West emphasize personal self-realization and the measurement of human worth in terms of individual productivity and power. This belief system causes older adults to see themselves as "beginning to fail" as they age, a phrase that refers as much to self-worth as it does to physical strength.

Theories and Views on Aging

An appreciation of the factors involved in the aging process and an understanding of the aging person are important to geriatric social work. Aging has several meanings. As a biological term, it is used to describe the inherent biological changes that occur over time and end with death.[2] People do not suddenly become old when they reach a certain birthday or milestone that we associate with entering "old age." Rather, aging is a gradual process that is shaped by a lifetime of experience. The content and complexity of the brain have grown over many years in the process of adapting, learning, and making memories. The aging person may have accumulated a variety of limitations from diseases, accidents, and life-style habits, but he or she is generally considered healthy if able to move without pain while completing activities of daily living.

As we look at other ways of thinking about aging, it is important to understand the older person in addition to the aging process. Increasingly, aging is seen from a life course perspective that looks at old age not as a separate period of life, but as a part of the total life course from birth to death.[3,4] In addition to describing the characteristics of old age that are attributed to biophysical changes, the framework of aging is expanded to include the complex interactions of age, social status, cohort effects, and history that impact an individual throughout all phases of his or her life. Life transitions, which may not be tied to a specific age or stage of life, are also a predictor of adaptation to old age. People who generally cope well with life transitions and role changes such as marriage, parenthood, retirement, and widowhood develop styles of coping that tend to remain intact. Erik Erikson, a noted developmental psychologist, described the life course as a series of psychological tasks, each requiring the person to resolve conflicting tendencies. In old age, Erikson identified the task as accepting one's life versus feeling hopeless and depressed about the limited time remaining—a conflict between ego-integrity and despair.[5]

Additional ways of looking at the aging process are through the activity and continuity theories of aging. The activity theory of aging assumes that the more active people are, the more likely they are to be happy. According to this theory, most older adults maintain the roles and activities established earlier in life because they continue to have the same needs and values in late life. The continuity theory of aging makes a similar point, noting that older adults are likely to maintain the same habits, personalities, and lifestyles they established in earlier years. According to both theories, any decreases in social interaction are more likely to be caused by poor health or disability than by a functional need of society to disengage older adults from their previous roles.[6] If retirement or age limitations make participation impossible, activity theory proposes that people will find substitutes for earlier roles or activities that had to be given up.

Older adults have been described as forgetful, rigid, irritable, and dependent, but there are a variety of ways in which individuals experience old age. Like member of any age group, older adults may experience anxiety, grief, or depression. It is important to separate out the personality traits demonstrated in earlier life, realistic responses to loss of friends and family, personal reactions to one's own aging and death, and the predictable emotional responses of human beings at any age to physical illness or social loss. The advantage of thinking in terms of age transitions is that adult development is seen as open-ended and an ongoing process. As a result, the meaning of old age is less fixed, and the choices older adults make are recognized as varied—an important challenge to the stereotypes that continue to persist about older adults.

Characteristics of the Older Adult Population

The older adult population can be described along several key dimensions, including the ratio of women to men, marital status, minority group membership, health and functioning, and economic status.

Sex and Gender

In terms of life expectancy, women live longer on average than men. Life expectancy for women in the United States is currently 81.1 years compared with 76.3 years for men.[7] As a result of women's greater life expectancy, there are more women than men aged 65-74 as well as women aged 85 and older.[8] This gender gap is found in almost every country where data are available. Because of these differences in life expectancy, women are more likely to be widowed in later life. Although most older adults have been married at some point in their lives, a majority (72%) of older women were widowed by age 85, whereas more than half of the men in that age group were still married. Women are also less likely to remarry, so when they require assistance later in life, they must depend on children or other relatives.

Health and Functioning

Research and clinical experience also suggest that old age may be subdivided at age 80. The health, psychological status, physical functioning, and response to medication of most people under the age of 80 (known as the "young-old") do not differ greatly from those of many middle-aged individuals. However, in people over 80 (the "old-old"), bodily functions deteriorate more rapidly, the risk of developing cognitive impairment increases, and the prevalence of illness is greater toward the end of life.

Most older adults under the age of 80 are in good health. Two-thirds rate their health as excellent or good, and 75% report no or only minor functional limitations in activities of daily living. Rates of disability, however, do increase with advancing age. The disability rate for those aged 85 and older is almost 6 times the rate of those aged 65–74. Among older adults aged 65–74 who reported a disability or limitation, some difficulty with independent living was the most prevalent disability (98%), followed by hearing loss (9%). Among people 85 and older, 48% reported having difficulty walking or climbing stairs. The second most common disability was difficulty doing errands, visiting a doctor's office, or shopping (43%). Hearing loss was third (35%).[8]

Influence of Culture and History on Older Adults

Aging takes place within a variety of cultures that shape not only the aging process, but also ideas about aging. These ideas include values, beliefs, norms, and stereotypes. Our values influence the desirability of different goals during various life stages. For an older adult in the United States, important goals associated with later life might be to maintain the ability to work or to retire and enjoy life. Beliefs are assertions of what is accepted as true and tell us about the nature of the reality in which values are based (e.g., for many Americans, career is believed to be a measure of accomplishment and is tied to important life transitions). Stereotypes are composites of several beliefs about a category of people, such as the widowed. Common stereotypes of widows may be that they are lonely, impoverished, and uninterested in romantic or sexual relationships.

These ideas about aging are not only shaped by culture, but also by the historical period in which we live. The year of birth shapes attitudes and values in late life and contributes to the prevalence and characteristics of emotional problems of that birth cohort. For example, the cohort of older adults born between 1900 and 1920 was found to have a lower prevalence of clinical depression and suicide than the preceding cohort or the cohort that immediately followed.[9]

Ethnic and Cultural Diversity Among Older Adults

Although the older population is largely white, older adults increasingly are ethnically and culturally diverse. Minority groups currently represent 23% of the 65-and-older population. By 2050, the United States Census Bureau projects that 30% of the 65-and-older population will be non-white, with the largest increase seen in the number of Hispanic older adults.[10]

In 2014, Hispanics—persons of Spanish descent from Central America, Latin America, Mexico, Cuba, and Puerto Rico—comprised 8% of the 65-and-older population in the United States. By 2060, it is projected that Hispanic individuals will comprise 21% of the 65-and-older population in the United States.[11]

Although there are some similarities among Hispanic ethnic groups in terms of culture, language, and experiences, there are also many differences across subgroups. For example, most Mexican Americans came to the United States to improve their economic status, whereas the majority of Cuban Americans immigrated for political and religious freedom. There are also individual differences within each Hispanic ethnic group in levels of acculturation to U.S. culture and language proficiency. Among other elder minority groups, the Hispanic population has the second-highest illiteracy rate and is most likely to live below the poverty line.[11]

The African American 65-and-older population consisted of 4 million people in 2014, representing 9% of the older population in the United States. That population is expected to grow to 12.8% by 2060.[12] The majority of today's African American elders are descendants of people who were brought involuntarily to the United States as slaves. As a group, African American elders are disadvantaged in several ways. In general, functional old age occurs at an earlier chronological age (e.g., 55 years) because of higher rates of disability and the accumulated effects of low education and financial disadvantages.

African American elders born in the early 1900s were raised during a period of tumultuous change for African Americans, including the civil rights movement and the ongoing fight against racism and discrimination. They saw many triumphs despite these trials, with African American achievements on the rise during this time. It is interesting to note that African Americans who survive to age 80 have lower mortality and morbidity rates than other racial and ethnic groups. Additionally, cultural practices indigenous to the African American community may protect elders from external stresses in old age. Stereotypes of African Americans in the United States often obscure the strengths of this group. African American elders are assumed to be living in unstable home and family environments. In reality, they typically have more frequent contact with and receive higher levels of social support from family members and their communities than their white counterparts.[13]

In 2014, Asian American elders accounted for 4% of the older population in the United States. By 2060, that percentage is expected to increase to 8%.[14] As an ethnic category, Asian American refers to any of 20-plus different Asian groups that include Chinese, Filipinos, Japanese, Koreans, and Southeast Asians. Although these groups may share some characteristics and values (e.g., the importance of family), there are significant differences as well, such as historical backgrounds, reasons for immigrating, and experiences in the United States. Although 85% of Asian elders were born outside the United States, many have lived most of their lives in this country. Yet, most are relatively unacculturated because they have resided in highly structured ethnic enclaves in which their customs and traditions have been maintained.[15]

The non-Hispanic American Indian, Alaska Native, and Native Hawaiian/Pacific Islander older population is referred to collectively as Native elders. In 2016, American Indians and Alaska Natives comprised 0.5% of the older population in the United States, with their numbers expected to grow to more than 630,000 by 2060. Native Hawaiians accounted for an additional 0.1%.[16]

Native American elders come from approximately 569 federally recognized tribes. Although there is a constant flux of Native Americans who move from reservations to urban areas, many return to reservations later in life. Each tribe has its own unique culture, language, beliefs, and customs.[17] Although age 65 is considered to be the beginning of old age in American society, there is no such consensus among Native tribes. In tribal communities, elders are considered the "wisdom-keepers" and are held in the highest regard.[18]

It is important to be mindful of the diversity among ethnic groups that results from different historical experiences. Not all members of

Hispanic, African American, Asian American, or Native American groups are similar, even though they may share a language, religion, or culture. People's experiences with racism and discrimination can also affect their response to social workers. Older adults of racial or ethnic minorities who request social work services may have already faced and overcome much adversity in their lives. Their experiences of discrimination, prejudice, and racism may affect how they respond to social institutions. Some may view social workers as authority figures and may be reluctant to share information.

Discrimination and prejudice do not only affect older adults—practicing social workers of racial or ethnic minorities may also be on the receiving end as well, as shown in the following story.

Not long after beginning my job as a medical social worker at Indian River Memorial Hospital in Vero Beach, Florida, I realized that many elements of racism were still evident in the rural South. The town's residents were predominately white, particularly those living along the beaches. Although much of the area's labor force was African American, many of these workers did not live in Vero Beach but resided in a small rural town a few miles to the north. Gifford was known for its acres of citrus groves and processing plants. The laborers who worked in the groves and nearby plants had established a community in which many of the hospital's African American employees lived. Small "cracker" houses lined the dirt roads, with a few wooden church buildings scattered throughout the community. As a young child living in Tennessee in the early 1950s, I had seen many African Americans living in poverty in the rural South, but I was not prepared to see similar situations 30 years later.

One of Gifford's residents, Carrie, worked as a social worker at the hospital. Carrie had received her bachelor's degree in social work at one of Florida's universities and had established a reputation at the hospital as a competent and caring social worker. It was Carrie who educated me about the unwritten rules of the segregated South.

It was Friday, typically a very busy day for social work staff because of the large number of patients to be discharged before the weekend. Carrie's caseload included the orthopedic patients, most of them older adults who had undergone hip or knee replacements or treatment for broken bones. As part of their discharge plans, it was necessary to order medical equipment, outpatient rehabilitation therapy, or in some cases, nursing home placement. A social work referral was received that morning, and I placed it on Carrie's desk.

Later that afternoon, Carrie came into my office to inform me that when she entered the patient's room, the older white woman had told her that she would only talk to a white social worker and not to a black one. My first reaction was one of anger directed toward the patient, followed by disbelief and sadness that racism was very much alive in our hospital and in our community. I apologized to Carrie and was surprised to hear that for her, this was part of her everyday life, and she had learned to deal with it.

―――――――――――

LGBTQ Older Adults

Although the needs of older adults who identify as lesbian, gay, bisexual, transgender, or queer (LGBTQ) are now recognized in the field of social work, LGBTQ adults are often considered as one group, with important distinctions between the different sexual orientations and sexual identities frequently overlooked. For example, bisexual men and women may feel marginalized by both heterosexual and homosexual communities. Transgender individuals often report experiencing significant bias and discrimination in healthcare encounters and have fewer legal protections than do gay, lesbian, and heterosexual adults. Some older gay men have watched many friends and others in the gay community die from the HIV/AIDS epidemic. Lesbians, in keeping with the gender differences in longevity, are more likely to face additional biases in long-term care settings.

It is estimated that 2.4 million LGBTQ older adults live in the United States, with the number expected to double by 2030.[19] Although research usually characterizes older adults as persons 65 years and older, LGBTQ persons who are over 50 tend to be characterized as being older in the literature. In 2015, more than 50% of people living with HIV/AIDS in the United States were older than 50, and with adults over 50 accounting for 1 in 6 new diagnoses, that number is projected to grow to 70% in 2020.[20]

Although the LGBTQ population has recently received some protections and rights in the United States, there is still little or no legal and social recognition of or support for LGBTQ relationships in some areas of the country. LGBTQ individuals continue to experience stigma and stereotypes resulting from homophobia, especially in old age. The marginalization of LGBTQ elders is apparent in the scarcity of institutional policies providing protections and the lack of attention this population receives from social service agencies and the medical community.[21]

Older lesbians, bisexual men and women, and gay men have a higher prevalence of mental health problems, disability, disease, and physical limitations than older heterosexual people. Transgender older adults are also at higher risk for poor physical health, disability, and depressive symptoms. However, despite the difficulties that many LGBTQ persons face in society, researchers have found that these challenges can foster coping skills that may be beneficial later in life. Older LGBTQ persons often report feeling a sense of competence as a result of early life crises surrounding the coming-out process. They also experience greater flexibility in cultural gender roles compared to heterosexuals and strong friendship networks.[22,23]

Disease and Disability

In addition to considering the social and cultural diversity of older adults, social workers should understand that individuals do not age at the same rate or experience the same health declines. Although physical changes occur as part of the aging process, such as sensory, musculoskeletal, respiratory, sexual, and skin changes, many health problems associated with aging are not necessarily caused by simply getting older. Age may be a risk factor for diseases such as heart disease, diabetes, stroke, Alzheimer's disease, and certain types of cancer, but genetics, lifestyle, and exposure to environmental toxins also play important roles in the development of these conditions.

Although many older adults live with chronic illnesses, these conditions may or may not limit their activities and lead to disability. Understanding and assessing functional ability is critical to aiding older adults and their families. When determining level of independence, it is important to consider the person's ability to perform daily-living tasks as well as his or her physical condition. The severity of functional disability is not only caused by physical impairments and their underlying medical conditions but also by external factors such as social and financial support and the environment. Geriatric social workers must be familiar with the psychological issues of aging and should pay attention to the interaction of physical and social problems. Some of the health problems associated with aging can potentially be modified by diet, exercise, change in personal habits, and social engagement.

Another important issue related to health and disability is the provision of care and support to older adults with intellectual and developmental disability (I/DD). Adults with I/DD are living into old age because of medical advances and improved living conditions, with this population expected to double from 641,860 in 2000 to 1.2 million by 2030.[24] As defined by the American Association on Intellectual and Developmental Disabilities, I/DD is characterized by significant limitations in both intellectual functioning and adaptive behavior, which covers many everyday social and practical skills. These disabilities originate before age 18.[23] People with such disabilities may have difficulty being fully independent in work, housing, and social settings, and this difficulty usually continues into old age. However, many individuals with I/DD are now supported to live and work in their communities.

The families of individuals with I/DD face unique challenges in providing care for their aging relatives. Adults with I/DD can have a shorter lifespan compared with other older adults, which is thought to be caused by an accelerated aging process. Older adults with I/DD have increased rates of cataracts, hearing loss, osteopenia, and hypothyroidism, along with a genetically elevated risk of developing Alzheimer's disease. They are also more likely to develop chronic health conditions at younger ages because of biological factors related to syndromes and associated developmental disabilities, limited access to adequate healthcare, lifestyle factors, and environmental issues. Individuals with I/DD experience higher rates of obesity, are more sedentary, and are more likely to have poor nutritional habits compared with members of the general population. As the life expectancy of individuals with I/DD increases and the transition from institutional care to family and community living continues, social workers and healthcare professionals will need to turn even more attention to the well-being and quality of life of older persons with I/DD.

To provide better care and support to older adults, our concept of aging should be adjusted so that we understand the diverse characteristics and abilities of this population. Extrinsic factors that affect the aging process, commonly thought to only facilitate the losses of aging, can play a neutral or even a positive role in the experience of growing older. The physical, psychological, and social functioning of older adults is just as varied as that of any age group across the lifespan.

CHAPTER NOTES

1. Osako, M. (1980). *Aging, social isolation and kinship ties among Japanese-Americans: Project report to the Administration on Aging.* Washington, DC: Administration on Aging.
2. Blazer, D. (1998). *Emotional problems in later life: Intervention strategies for professional caregivers* (2nd ed.). New York: Springer Publishing Company.
3. Moody, H.R. (2010). *Aging concepts and controversies.* Los Angeles: Pine Forge Press.
4. Marks, E.W., & Hollis-Sawyer, L.A. (Eds.) (2000). *Intersections of aging: Readings in social gerontology.* Los Angeles: Roxbury Publishing Company.
5. Costa, P.T., Jr., & McCrae, R.R. (1980). Still stable after all these years: Personality as a key to some issues in aging. In P.B. Baltes & O.G. Brim (Eds.), *Life-span development and behavior* (Vol. 3) (pp. 65–102). New York: Academic Press.
6. Havighurst, R.J., Neugarten, B.L., & Tobin, S.S. (1968). Disengagement and patterns of aging. In B.L. Neugarten (Ed.), *Middle age and aging* (pp 161–172). Chicago: University of Chicago Press.
7. Arias, E., & Xu, J. (2019). United States life tables, 2017. *National Vital Statistics Reports, 68* (7), 1. Retrieved from https://www.cdc.gov/nchs/data/nvsr/nvsr68/nvsr68_07-508.pdf
8. Roberts, A.W., Ogunwole, S.U., Blakeslee, L., & Rabe, M.A. (2018). *The population 65 years and older in the United States: 2016* (American Community Survey Reports, ACS-38). Washington, DC: U.S. Census Bureau.
9. Centers for Disease Control and Prevention National Center for Health Statistics (2016) *Healthy aging in action: Advancing the national prevention strategy.* Retrieved from https://cdc.gov/aging/pdf/healthy -aging-in-action508.pdf.
10. Ortman, J.M., Velkoff, V.A., & Hogan, H. (2014). *An aging nation: The older population in the United States: Population estimates and projections* (P25-1140). Washington, DC: U.S. Department of Commerce, U.S. Census Bureau. Retrieved from https://www.census.gov/content/dam/Census/library/publications/2014/demo/p25-1140.pdf
11. Administration for Community Living. (2017) *2017 profile of Hispanic Americans age 65 and older.* Washington, DC: U.S. Department of Health and Human Services. Retrieved from https://acl.gov/sites/default/files/Aging and Disability in America/2017OAProfileHA508.pdf
12. Administration for Community Living. (2018). *2017 profile of African Americans age 65 and over.* Washington, DC: U.S. Department of Health and Human Services. Retrieved from https://acl.gov/sites/default/files/Aging and Disability in America/2017OAProfileAfAm508.pdf
13. For further reading on African American elders, see George, L. (1988). Social participation in later life: Black-white differences. In J.S. Jackson (Ed.), *The Black American elderly: Research on physical and psychosocial health.* New York: Springer Publishing Company; Taylor, R.J. (1988). Aging and supportive relationships among Black Americans. In J.S. Jackson (Ed.), *The Black American elderly: Research on physical and psychosocial health.* New York: Springer Publishing Company.
14. Administration for Community Living. (2018). *2017 profile of Asian Americans age 65 and over.* Washington, DC: U.S. Department of Health and Human Services. Retrieved from https://acl.gov/sites/default/files/Aging and Disability in America/2017OAProfileAsAm508.pdf

15. National Asian Pacific Center on Aging. (2010) *Asian Americans and Pacific Islanders in the United States aged 65 years and older: Population, nativity, and language.* Data Brief 1(3). Retrieved from https://www.napca.org/wp-content/uploads/2017/10/65-population -report-FINAL.pdf

16. Administration for Community Living. (2017) *Profile of American Indians and Alaska Natives age 65 and over.* Washington, DC: U.S. Department of Health and Human Services. Retrieved from https://acl.gov/sites/default/files/Aging and Disability in America/2017OAProfileAIAN508.pdf

17. National Congress of American Indians (NCAI). (2015). *Tribal nations and the United States: An introduction.* Retrieved from http://www.ncai.org/tribalnations/introduction /Tribal_Nations_and_the_United_States_An_Introduction-web-.pdf

18. Whitewater, S., Reinschmidt, K.M., Kahn, C., Attakai, A., Teufel-Shone, N.I. (2016) Flexible roles for American Indian elders in community-based participatory research. *Preventing Chronic Disease, 23,* E72.

19. Choi, S.K., & Meyer, I.H. (2016). *LGBTQ aging: A review of research findings, needs, and policy implications.* Los Angeles: The Williams Institute. Retrieved from https:// williamsinstitute.law.ucla.edu/wp-content/uploads/LGBTQ-Aging-A-Review.pdf

20. Tax, A. (2015, September 28). On National HIV/Aging Awareness Day: Alarming statistics [Blog post]. Retrieved from https://www.sageusa.org/recognizing-national -hivaging-awareness-day/

21. Berger, R.M. (1982). *Gay and gray.* Urbana, IL: University of Illinois Press.

22. Friend, R.A. (1987). The individual and social psychology of aging: Clinical implications for lesbians and gay men. *Journal of Homosexuality, 14,* 307–331.

23. Heller, T. (2014). People with intellectual and developmental disabilities growing old: An overview. *Impact, 23*(1), 2–3.

24. American Association on Intellectual and Developmental Disabilities (AAIDD). (2019). Definition of intellectual disability. Retrieved from https://aaidd.org /intellectual-disability/definition. For further reading on older adults with intellectual and developmental disabilities, see Heller, T., Stafford, P.B., Davis, L.A., & Sedlezky, L. (Eds.) (2010). Feature issue on aging and people with intellectual and developmental disabilities. *Impact, 23*(1), 1–36. Retrieved from https://ici.umn .edu/products/impact/231/231.pdf; Bittles, A., Petterson, B.A., Sullivan, S.G., Hussain, R., Glasson, E.J., & Montgomery, P.D. (2002).The influence of intellectual disability on life expectancy. *The Journals of Gerontology Series A: Biological Science and Medical Science, 57,* 470–472; Janicki, M.P., Dalton, A.J., Henderson, C.M., & Davidson, P.W. (1999). Mortality and morbidity among older adults with intellectual disability: Health services considerations. *Disability and Rehabilitation, 21*(5–6), 284–294.

CHAPTER 3

Skills and Personal Resources of the Social Worker

KEY POINTS

- Our self-perception affects how we interact with and behave toward others.

- Developing cultural competency in geriatric social work practice requires an understanding of the role that race, ethnicity, and culture play in influencing the life events of older adults.

- Role transitions that occur during the aging process may diminish an older person's sense of self.

TO UNDERSTAND AND HELP OTHERS, it is necessary to have a sense of self. Self-concept, defined by Judith Viorst as a "declaration of a consciousness of self," makes us aware of who we are and how we came to be who we are. As social workers, we need to develop a strong awareness of self and learn to accept both our strengths and our vulnerabilities.[1]

Understanding the Self-Concept

To develop a better understanding of self-concept, it is helpful to acknowledge the impact of loss on ourselves and others, as well as other influences that shape how people think, feel, and respond to life changes. Examples of these early influences on self-concept include parents, family, friends, and school. Depending on the individual's experience, these factors can be considered ego boosters or ego busters. Our ego states, a system of feelings and related behaviors, are influenced by our environment and a learned

Table 3.1 Ego States

Ego State	Attributes
Parent ego state	Comes from parental figures
	Responds with same posture, gestures, vocabulary, and feelings as parent(s)
Child ego state	Is fixed in early childhood (creativity, enjoyment)
Adult ego state	Is directed toward objective appraisal of reality
	Processes data and computes probabilities essential for dealing with the outside world
	Regulates activities of parent and child states

repertoire of psychological realities that we acquire throughout life. Table 3.1 presents the three main ego states, each associated with a particular set of behaviors, postures, viewpoints, vocabulary, intentions, and reactions.[2]

How we interact with and behave toward others depends on our perception of self and others. Self-perception has been explained in various ways, but the basic components first appeared in the Tennessee Self-Concept Scale. Knowing these components can help us understand our older clients' perception of self.[3]

Physical Self

In our youth-oriented culture, the loss of a youthful image and the transition into later life may be very stressful for some people. Even healthy older adults are usually dissatisfied with their physical selves. They complain about the loss of energy, muscular strength, and flexibility, as well as changes in vision, hearing, and memory. Older adults with illness or disability have an even more negative perception of their physical self. Declining health affects an individual's sense of independence and often results in a loss of control and choices.

Moral-Ethical Self

The moral-ethical character of the older adult may be a reflection of an earlier era and might conflict with current lifestyles and values. Moral standards that were taught and reinforced during a person's early years may influence his or her perception of current social practices. Negative views of the lifestyles led by younger generations may result in disengagement and loneliness.

Personal Self

Age can also diminish the personal self. As we age, our daily routine and social roles involving our occupations, marriage, family, and community status gradually evolve into new life situations. New roles and a new self-concept need to be defined and developed as a person transitions into older adulthood. Role transitions that accompany the aging process may be stressful for older adults. The inability to cope successfully with life changes, such as retirement, widowhood, bereavement, or isolation, places an individual at risk for developing a stress-related emotional or physical reaction.

Family Self

Within the family system, older adults usually experience changes in roles. They may find themselves in the role of caregiver to a partner, spouse, sibling, parent, child, or grandchild. Four-generation families are becoming increasingly common, with an adult child simultaneously providing care to an aging parent(s) and his or her children.

Social Self

An older adult's perception of the social self is affected by how society views and cares for its older population. The media often presents disproportionately positive or negative views of older adults. One-dimensional stories often feature older adults with unusual successes or physical stamina, characteristics that are not representative of most older adults. On the other hand, television commercials have presented negative stereotypes of older adults through the use of older actors to sell laxatives, wrinkle removers, adult diapers, and prescription medications. These advertisements and media perceptions present the idea that older adults are in failing health and losing their dignity, vitality, and youthful attractiveness.

Self-Reflection and Cultural Competency in the Social Work Profession

Once we have developed an awareness of the self and an understanding of the lifelong influences that have shaped our beliefs, values, and how we interact with others, we can begin to see older adults as individuals who have also been influenced by life events that affect how they feel, behave, and respond to changes and challenges. Social workers who are on a path of self-discovery must also develop an understanding of the role that race, ethnicity, and culture play in their lives and in the lives of others (i.e., cultural competency). Our understanding of these identities has evolved, as discussed in a 2014 article published in *The New Social Worker*:

> Race is a social construct (American Anthropological Association, 1998) with the sole intention of separation and power based on the color of one's skin. More accurate terms of ethnicity and ethnic origin have begun to emerge, not to displace the term of "race," but rather to highlight a significant component of ethnic and national origin. Because of the impact "race" has had on society, it continues to be a necessary concept to acknowledge as the profession takes the journey toward fully embracing racial and ethnic identity.[4]

To serve others and better understand identity formation, social workers must develop self-awareness, including the acknowledgment of one's own racial and ethnic identity. Knowing who we are influences how we interact with others. Carolyne Rodriguez, LCSW and retired Texas State Strategy Director of Casey Family Programs, stated, "If they [social workers] are to effectively promote racial and ethnic pride with clients and are to demonstrate an understanding of the importance of culture, race, and ethnicity, this starts with knowing themselves."[4] For white social workers, this means that they have to acknowledge a historical reality that is filled with acts of discrimination based on power and privilege. Institutional and individual acts of racism may be uncomfortable for both white individuals and persons of color to acknowledge, but it is necessary to learn about the history of racism and its influence on social workers and the persons with whom they interact.

Here are two exercises that I used in my classes to help students develop a perspective of "self-concept" and to identify the important influences in their lives.

Relational Effectiveness Activity

Instructions:

1. List 20 characteristics that describe how you perceive yourself and how you believe others perceive you (e.g., ambitious, cautious, critical, direct, emotional, impulsive, understanding).

2. Rank the characteristics you selected from most important to least important.

3. Place a check by those characteristics you perceive as positive.

Discussion:

- How do these characteristics affect your interpersonal communication?

- Do you believe that others share this view of you? (Ask family and friends to name several characteristics and compare others' views to your perceptions.)

- How do these characteristics relate to your beliefs about yourself?

Lifeline Map Activity

Instructions:

1. On a large sheet of paper or poster board, draw the lifeline that is etched in the palm of your hand, extending the line across the paper.

2. At the lower point of the lifeline, mark your date of birth. Based on average life expectancy and other factors, estimate how long you might live and mark that age and date at the upper end of the lifeline. Place an "X" on the line where you are today.

3. Note the following on your lifeline, marking the date on which each experience occurred or when you estimate an event will occur in the future:

   - Meeting the most influential people in your life

   - Significant events and decisions in your life

   - Future plans

Discussion:

- Who were the most influential people in your life, and how did they affect your life course (positive or negative effects/ego boosters or ego busters)?

- Which events and decisions in your life had the most significance in your life course (positive or negative effects/ego boosters or ego busters)?

- What are your plans for the future?

- What are the reasons for your projected end of lifespan?

Getting in touch with oneself can be very useful for social work practice. When we explore our own life experiences and values, it helps us to understand that a person's self-concept or self-perception is often shaped by a few important people and events, both positively and negatively. The two exercises I assigned to social work students helped them understand their self-concept and the influences that affected their sense of self. These influences can also play a role in how we feel about and behave toward our clients. Factors that influence our perceptions of others include the following:

- Past experiences

- Relational satisfaction

- Assumptions about human behavior

- Expectations

- Knowledge

- Personal mood

An individual who reaches the later stages of life is the product of many life stages and challenges, as shared by the poem "A Crabbit Old Woman Wrote This," which was written by a hospital nurse in Scotland.[5]

A Crabbit Old Woman Wrote This

What do you see, nurses, what do you see:

Are you thinking when you look at me—

A crabbit old woman, not very wise,

Uncertain of health, with far-away eyes,

Who dribbles her food and makes no reply

When you say in a loud voice
"I do wish you'd try."
Who seems not to notice the things that you do,
And forever is losing a stocking or shoe.
Who unresisting or not, lets you do as you will,
With bathing and feeding, the long day to fill.
Is that what you're thinking, is that what you see?
Then open your eyes, nurse, you're not looking at me.
I'll tell you who I am as I sit here so still,
As I rise at your bidding, as I eat at your will.
I'm a small child of ten with a father and mother,
Brothers and sisters, who love one another;
A young girl of sixteen with wings on her feet,
Dreaming that soon now a lover I'll meet;
A bride soon at twenty—my heart gives a leap,
Remembering the vows that I promised to keep;
At twenty-five now I have young of my own,
Who need me to build a secure happy home;
A woman of thirty, my young now grow fast,
Bound to each other with ties that should last;
At forty, my young sons have grown and are gone,
But my man's beside me to see I don't mourn;
At fifty once more babies play round my house,
Again we know children, my loved one and me.
Dark days are upon me, my husband is dead,
I look at the future, I shudder with dread.
For my young are all rearing young of their own.
And I think of the years and the love that I've known
I'm an old woman now and nature is cruel—
Tis her jest to make old age look like a fool.
The body is crumbled, grace and vigor depart,
There now is a stone where I once had a heart.
But inside this old carcass a young girl still dwells,

And now and again my battered heart swells.

I remember the years, I remember the pain,

And I'm loving and living life over again.

I think of the years all too few—gone too fast,

And accept the stark fact that nothing can last.

So open your eyes, nurses, open and see

Not a crabbit old woman, look close—see ME.

By Phyllis McCormack, a Scottish nurse, in Nursing Mirror, *December 1972.*[5]

Social Work Skills

With the expansion of mental health coverage under Medicare in the late 1980s, many people who did not have training or experience in geriatrics were pressed into providing services for older adults. This was especially true in long-term care settings, where many mental health professionals had been working without much understanding or knowledge of clinical issues in later life. This situation led to the development of standards for training in geriatric mental health. In 1981, the NASW developed *Standards for Social Work Services in Long-Term Care Facilities.*[6] The American Psychiatric Association and the American Psychological Association also developed guidelines for training and experience.

Most social service professionals working with older adults received little or no training relevant to aging. This does not imply that these practicing social workers need to start from scratch to become geriatric specialists. Social workers already possess basic skills in communication, assessment, and problem-solving. However, these professionals can benefit from additional training that includes knowledge about common illnesses and disorders affecting older people, the distinct manifestations of illnesses in older clients, a broad-based multidisciplinary approach to working with aging clients, and an attitude and awareness that facilitate work with older adults.

Communication Skills

Successful communication with older adults requires recognizing that they are individuals with the right to choose and act independently regardless of any physical or cognitive limitations. Effective communication requires

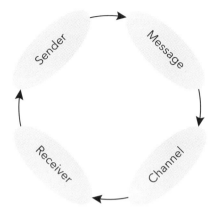

Figure 3.1   The Communication Process

a two-way process.[7] Figure 3.1 displays a simplified flow of communication. The sender is the person who communicates the original message. The message can be either verbal or nonverbal (e.g., communication through facial expression, tone of voice, behavior, gestures, and so forth). The channel is the medium (e.g., acoustic, visual, electronic) through which the message is transmitted. The receiver is the person or persons receiving the message.

In most situations, the steps of the communication process happen almost simultaneously, with the receiver translating the message and responding to the sender within moments. However, some older adults may have physical and medical conditions that create barriers to effective communication, such as ill-fitting dentures, hearing loss, aphasia, agnosia, apraxia, and dementia. These factors can all cause a breakdown in the two-way communication process. The social worker may need to adapt his or her communication efforts to help overcome such barriers and facilitate the process.

Assessment Skills

Assessment is the most important clinical skill in social work practice with older adults because it is the foundation upon which intervention strategies and treatment goals are developed. Geriatric social workers must know how to assess for dementia, delirium, depression, and other common disorders of later life and differentiate these disorders from normal effects of aging. An assessment is a critical evaluation of the older person in his or her environment and is a summary of an individual's presenting strengths and problems or needs. This process requires knowledge of normal aging, aging disorders, and a multifaceted evaluation process.[8] Using an interdisciplinary perspective, social workers provide a comprehensive view of the person that includes nonmedical, social, and emotional considerations.

Problem-Solving Skills

Problem solving is a practice model used by social workers to help clients meet their therapy goals. Rather than tell clients what to do, social workers teach clients how to apply a problem-solving method so they can develop their own solutions. Because older adults may experience everyday stressors related to medical illnesses, losses, disability, and cognitive impairment, a hands-on approach using discrete and easily taught steps to solve problems is practical and effective. Cognitive skills involved in the initiation, planning, and organization of goal-directed behavior may decline in aging and, to a further extent, with the progression of dementia. Older adults with cognitive impairment often require additional compensatory strategies, such as written notes, memory devices, environmental adaptations, and caregiver involvement.

Older adults can teach us much about the aging experience. Most of what I know about aging has been taught to me by older people: clients, patients, relatives, and friends.

A career with older adults can also be challenging because this work can raise very personal issues and concerns about our own future. Geriatric social work allows us to work with wonderful role models who exhibit tremendous strength and wisdom, but we are also faced with the enormous struggles of older adults living with physical, emotional, and financial hardships. If older adults have difficulty understanding and navigating their own experiences related to aging or other life challenges, then it is up to the social worker to help clients make sense of their challenges, draw conclusions, articulate the patterns, and find solutions.

CHAPTER NOTES

1. Viorst, J. (1998). *Necessary losses*. New York: Simon & Schuster.
2. Berne, E. (1961). *Transactional analysis in psychotherapy*. New York: Grove Press.
3. Fitts, W.H. (1972). *The self-concept and performance* (Research Monograph, 5). Nashville: The Dede Wallace Center.
4. Hall, E., & Lindsey, S. (2014, Summer). Teaching cultural competence: A closer look at racial and ethnic identity formation. *The New Social Worker, 21*(3), 4–5. Retrieved from https://www.socialworker.com/feature-articles/ethics-articles /teaching-cultural-competence/
5. Searle, C. (1973). *Elders*. UK: Reality Press.
6. National Association of Social Workers (NASW). (2003). *Standards for social work services in long-term care facilities*. Washington, DC: NASW.
7. Dreher, B.B. (2001). *Communication skills for working with others*. New York: Springer Publishing Company.
8. For further reading on assessment, see Zarit, S.H., & Zarit, J.M. (2007). *Mental disorders in older adults: Fundamentals of assessment and treatment*. New York: Guilford Press; Zuckerman, E.L. (2000). *Clinician's thesaurus*. New York: Guilford Press; Kane, R.A., & Kane, R. (1981). *Assessing the elderly: A practical guide to measurement*. Lexington, MA: Lexington Books.

CHAPTER 4

Ethical Issues in Social Work Practice with Older Adults

KEY POINTS

- Social work ethics are rooted in the core values of social work. These include service, social justice, client dignity and worth, importance of human relationships, integrity, and competence.

- Ethical dilemmas specific to the practice and treatment of older adults present challenges for the social worker.

- The distinction between mental competency and rationality should be considered in the determination of an individual's decision-making ability.

AGING IS A COMPLICATED PROCESS that requires complex decisions and raises a number of ethical considerations related to the care and treatment of older adults in society. Several critical factors play a role in decisions about the care of older adults:

- The growing population of older adults

- The scarcity and high costs of health resources

- An increase in the number of persons with chronic diseases and disabilities

- Society's stereotypes of older people as being dependent, sick, and confused (i.e., ageism)

In most geriatric treatment settings, healthcare and social service providers practice in the interests of their clients. In research and in managed care, they serve other interests as well, such as funding sources and organizational directives. Given a finite number of resources, cost control will continue to be a concern for the client, provider, and the public at large. When working with older adults, social workers should also respect privacy, self-determination, and the maintenance of independence for as long as possible.

Self-Determination

Older adults, like persons of all ages, value autonomy. In some cases, the line between independence and self-neglect is thin, and social workers must be careful not to infringe on older adults' right to live as they wish. In our society, the ethical foundation for requiring consent before testing, treatment, or care is personal autonomy, a person's right to self-determination and to make his or her own choices.

Common examples of an older adult's expression of autonomy would be refusing care or treatment, insisting on receiving care or treatment, or insisting on remaining in the home. The opposite of autonomy is paternalism, or the interference with a person's right to choose for the good of either the individual, family, care provider, institution, or society. Paternalism includes failing to include an older adult in decision-making or failing to provide the information needed to make decisions. The ethical issue of self-determination can affect geriatric care in several ways:

- The persons involved in decisions related to the health and well-being of older persons may have conflicting philosophies, values, and motives.

- A person's ability to make decisions is dependent on his or her knowledge and understanding of the assessment and the resulting treatment or plan for services. This information may be confusing for some older adults.

- A person's ability to make decisions is tied to his or her level of mental competence.

Additionally, a distinction must be made between competency and rationality when working with clients. A person can be legally competent to make decisions that may not be rational. A decision may be considered irrational if it has the potential to be harmful or to increase the likelihood of death, pain, disability, or loss of freedom and opportunity. Social workers should consider several criteria when assessing the decision-making abilities of older adults and determining if their consent is valid:

- Is the person's decision being influenced by others that he or she depends on for care, finances, housing, or other services?
- Is the person's refusal to comply with an assessment or testing based on a fear of the results, which may lead to a loss of independence or control?
- Have choices been made available when possible?
- Has coercion been used, such as threats or depriving the individual of rights or freedom?
- Has the older person received adequate information about the proposed procedure, plan of treatment, or plan of care?
- Is the older person mentally competent to make the decision?

In the early days of hospital social work, most referrals for social work services involved discharge planning and working with patients' families. Physician referrals for social work counseling on health-related decisions and issues were infrequent despite the benefits that counseling provided to patients. In the following account, I describe a time when I received pushback from a physician for speaking with a patient about his concerns related to death and dying.

The year was 1981, and I was making my rounds on the hospital's oncology unit when a nurse approached me and said that one of her cancer patients had asked to talk to a social worker. The patient's physician had not made a referral, but because I was assigned to cover patients on this unit, I agreed to speak with the patient and made my way to his room. Before entering the patient's room, I glanced at his medical chart and saw that the 70-year-old patient had been diagnosed with late-stage pancreatic cancer. I entered the dark room, and the patient, Edward, greeted me from his bed, his voice weak and barely audible. I introduced myself and mentioned that his nurse had asked me to see him.

"Yes, I need to talk to someone," Edward responded. I pulled a chair up close to the bed and leaned over so that I could hear him. "You see, I'm dying, and no one will talk to me about it. My family tells me that I will get better, and they change the subject whenever I try to talk about my illness. When my doctor comes to see me, he doesn't stay very long or answer my questions."

I explained that although I was unable to answer his questions about his medical condition, I would be glad to listen to his concerns. For the next 30 minutes, I sat with Edward while he talked about his life and his feelings about his impending death. "Thank you for listening to me," Edward said as I got up to leave. Outside his room, I opened his medical chart and documented my visit, writing, "Patient discussed his concerns about dying. Supportive counseling was provided."

The next day, I received a call from the hospital administrator asking me to come to his office. When I arrived, he informed me that Edward's physician had stormed into his office that morning and issued a complaint against me for "talking to my patient about dying." Edward's family had decided not to tell him that his condition was terminal and asked his physician to go along with their wishes. I explained to the administrator that the patient had acknowledged that he was dying and that he wanted to talk about it with someone because he could not discuss it with his family or physician. I also reminded the administrator that, as a social worker, my priority was the welfare of my patient, who, in this case, was Edward.

This was a situation in which the family was uncomfortable addressing the patient's terminal condition and was having difficulty accepting the reality of impending death, and the patient was aware that he was dying but could not discuss it. As a result, everyone danced around the issue. The hospital administrator supported me in this case. Edward died the following week.

———————————

Death and dying should be understood in the context of other cultures as well as the social worker's own. Many cultures and religions have distinct traditions and behaviors associated with death and dying. Social workers should learn about the traditions of their clients' cultures to help older adults deal with the death of friends and family and with their own end-of-life experience. In the following story, I share a situation that demonstrates conflict between providers' values and individual choice.

I looked up from my desk to see a young woman standing in the doorway to my office. She hesitated for a moment, then asked to talk to a social worker about her mother, Rose, who was a patient in the hospital's intensive care unit (ICU). I was covering the ICU that day, so I invited her to sit down and listened as she explained her mother's situation.

Rose had been taken to the emergency room the previous day and was admitted to the ICU by the hospital's on-call neurologist, who had placed her on a respirator. Diagnosed in her late 40s with myasthenia gravis, a progressive autoimmune disorder, Rose had been receiving care from a home health agency for many years. Her daughter, who lived in another state, had received a call from the agency alerting her that her mother's condition had worsened. When she arrived in town, she learned that Rose had been taken to the hospital. As she relayed her concerns, Rose's daughter expressed frustration about the disregard for her mother's wishes shown by the hospital's neurologist. She explained that when her mother first learned about her diagnosis and her prognosis, she completed a living will stating that when she entered the terminal phase of her illness and could no longer breathe on her own, she did not want to prolong her life by artificial means. She further explained that her mother was Asian and that her wishes were in accordance with her cultural beliefs and traditions. The daughter's sense of frustration turned to anger when she told me that, even though a copy of Rose's living will had been placed in her medical chart, the neurologist was still refusing to honor it because removing Rose from the respirator was against his religious beliefs.

As I entered Rose's cubicle in the ICU, I was struck by the silence, broken only by the muted sounds of the machines that were monitoring her vital signs and keeping her alive. Rose was motionless in the bed—the disease had not only affected the respiratory muscles that controlled her breathing, but also had caused paralysis in her limbs as well as her facial and eye muscles. Unable to speak, Rose responded to my questions by opening and closing her eyelids. When I asked her if she wanted to remain connected to the respirator, she closed her eyes briefly to indicate "no," then stared at me as tears rolled down her cheeks.

Making notes in her medical chart, I flipped to the front of the binder and found her living will. My next step was to meet with the hospital administrator. I explained Rose's situation and that her wishes regarding treatment, as expressed in her living will, were not being honored by her physician. To my dismay, the administrator agreed with her physician's decision, telling me that he held similar religious beliefs against the removal of life-support. Had this situation taken place several years later, there would have been new laws affecting a person's end-of-life choices that would have made it easier for Rose to have her wishes respected.

I was not ready to give up in my efforts to help Rose. When I met with her daughter the next morning, I explained the legal process she would need to go through to take her mother off the respirator. She was able to obtain guardianship through the court and, as Rose's guardian, terminated the services of the neurologist and brought in a new physician who honored Rose's wishes and took her off the respirator. This was not the first time, nor would it be the last, that I would have to walk the tightrope between adherence to organizational rules and client advocacy.

There are many instances in social work when there are no simple answers to resolve complex ethical issues. Situations may arise in which social workers' ethical obligations conflict with organizational policies, relevant laws, or regulations. When these conflicts occur, social workers must make a responsible effort to resolve the conflict in a manner that is consistent with the values, principles, and standards expressed in the *NASW Code of Ethics*:

> The primary mission of the social work profession is to enhance human well-being and help meet the basic human needs of all people, with particular attention to the needs and empowerment of people who are vulnerable, oppressed, and living in poverty. A historic and defining feature of social work is the profession's focus on individual well-being in a social context and the well-being of society. Fundamental to social work is attention to the environmental forces that create, contribute to, and address problems in living.
>
> Social workers promote social justice and social change with and on behalf of clients. "Clients" is used inclusively to refer to

individuals, families, groups, organizations, and communities. Social workers are sensitive to cultural and ethnic diversity and strive to end discrimination, oppression, poverty, and other forms of social injustice. These activities may be in the form of direct practice, community organizing, supervision, consultation, administration, advocacy, social and political action, policy development and implementation, education, and research and evaluation. Social workers seek to enhance the capacity of people to address their own needs. Social workers also seek to promote the responsiveness of organizations, communities, and other social institutions to individuals' needs and social problems.

The mission of the social work profession is rooted in a set of core values. These core values, embraced by social workers throughout the profession's history, are the foundation of social work's unique purpose and perspective:

- Service
- Social justice
- Dignity and worth of the person
- Importance of human relationships
- Integrity
- Competence[1]

Confidentiality

When social workers coordinate care for older adults, they must share client information with families, other professionals, and service providers. This often presents an ethical challenge as the social worker attempts to balance the protection of the client's right to privacy and autonomy with the need to provide necessary information to ensure appropriate care is delivered.

Intake and assessment are the initial steps in the development of an intervention and treatment plan and involve obtaining information about clients and their families. Included in this information are demographics such as age, religion, residence, and financial circumstances, as well as a psychosocial and medical history. Facts about the client's financial situation are especially important because economic status can be a significant criterion for eligibility in many programs and settings.

Most programs require clients to sign a form consenting to an exchange of information among providers. The Health Insurance Portability and Accountability Act of 1996 (HIPAA; PL 104-191) provides data privacy and security provisions for safeguarding medical information. For the release of medical information, a HIPAA form is now required to be signed by the client or his or her representative.[2] Typically, a client signs a HIPAA release form without fully understanding how widely the information collected will be shared. This raises the possibility that informed consent has not taken place.

An assessment begins with the client as the primary source of information, then turns to family and others for additional information as needed, such as in the case of a client's questionable or lack of mental capacity. Initial contact with the client is important not only for obtaining relevant data, but also for protecting the client's basic rights of privacy and self-determination. A distrust of the healthcare and social service systems and the fear that any information obtained will be used against them can be obstacles to completing an accurate assessment of older persons. Older clients may hesitate to disclose personal information that could indicate a need for support services or long-term care placement and possibly result in the loss of control and independence. The following case exemplifies a social worker's dilemma in respecting a client's right to privacy and self-determination:

Helen was an 86-year-old woman who lived alone in a single-family house. Although she had resided in the neighborhood for 35 years, many of her neighbors had died or moved away, and she had no support system nearby. Her only child, a son, lived in another state and visited her infrequently. Concerned about the deteriorating condition of Helen's house, a neighbor contacted the county aging services program. The social worker who visited Helen to assess her situation found her to be frail but mentally competent and extremely distrustful of others. Although she allowed the social worker to contact her son, Helen refused to agree to the release of personal information to any third party. The social worker concluded that Helen's goal to remain in her home was feasible despite objections from both her son and the neighbor who contacted the agency. A care plan was implemented that included home repair, housekeeping services, and monthly visits by the social worker.

Confidentiality is a legal and moral right of individuals derived from the right of privacy and reinforced by the *NASW Code of Ethics*.[1] However, ethical dilemmas arise when the right to confidentiality and the need to prioritize the client's best interest and welfare are in conflict. Challenges often faced by social workers include clients' cognitive impairments and the loss of mental capacity, which may deprive clients of the ability to make decisions on their own behalf. In that situation, care of the person is arranged through a third party, usually a family member, guardian, attorney, or bank trust officer.

Over the past 30 years, societal views on confidentiality have changed from confidentiality being an absolute right to a relative one. Today, a person's confidentiality can be waived or overruled in certain circumstances if believed to be for the welfare of the individual or the good of society.[3] First, private information can be disclosed without client consent to protect the client. For example, confidentiality may be overridden when the life or safety of the client is endangered because of injury or neglect, either self-imposed or by another person. Another exception to the right of confidentiality occurs when social workers are required by a court of law to release information. The ability to waive confidentiality in certain circumstances carries a risk, however, potentially causing professionals to view older adults in a patronizing way or leading to premature intervention. Social workers must always carefully balance the protection and well-being of the client with upholding the rights of confidentiality, as violation of these rights risks damage to the older adult's sense of privacy and self-esteem. Professionals working with older adults should take several steps to help protect their confidentiality:

- View client records as potential public documents. Balancing client privacy with appropriately informing third parties is often a challenge.

- Have consent forms signed by the client or a legal representative before disclosing information about that client.

- Discuss with the client (or the client's legal representative) what information he or she is comfortable having shared with family, friends, and other members of the client's informal support system.

- If the communication of client information is mandated by law, inform clients that they still have the right to know under what conditions their names and case information will be shared.

- Include guidelines for maintaining client confidentiality in contracts between service providers.

- Explain the limits of confidentiality to clients.

The ethical dilemma of balancing the welfare of the client with client rights and autonomy will likely only become more complex over time within the social work profession. As we continue to see increased life expectancy for older adults, the potential for conflicting interests between the needs of older people and the values and ethics of people who attempt to meet those needs will grow.

CHAPTER NOTES

1. The National Association of Social Workers (NASW). (2017). *Code of ethics of the National Association of Social Workers.* Retrieved from https://www.socialworkers.org/About/Ethics/Code-of-Ethics/Code-of-Ethics-English

2. Office for Civil Rights (OCR). (2017). HIPAA for professionals. Retrieved from https://www.hhs.gov/hipaa/for-professionals/index.html

3. For further reading on guidelines for confidentiality, see Zarit, S.H., & Zarit, J.M. (2007). *Mental disorders in older adults.* New York: The Guilford Press; Knight, B.G. (1999). *Psychotherapy with older adults.* Thousand Oaks, CA: SAGE Publications; Kaplan, M. (1999). Case management and confidentiality. *Journal of Ethics, Law, and Aging, 5*(2), 103–110; Bergmark, R., & Parker, M. (1998). How confidential is confidential? *Managed Care and Aging, 5*(1), 1–10.

CHAPTER 5

Effective Counseling Theories and Orientations

KEY POINTS

- Counseling can address the issues and problems of later life and help older adults to live a fulfilling and productive life.

- Understanding traditional aging theories can enable social workers to make evidence-based practice decisions and use effective interventions that improve the lives of older adults.

- Changing demographics, changes in physical and psychological functioning, cultural diversity, and changes in family structure affect practice approaches and work with older adults.

SOCIAL WORK WITH OLDER ADULTS requires a multifaceted approach. Clinicians need to draw on basic skills of psychotherapy; coordinate psychological treatment with psychiatric and other medical treatment; and intervene at different levels with clients, their families, and other people involved in the care of older adults, modifying approaches or the therapeutic environment as needed.

Techniques for Effectively Communicating with Older Adults

The success of any treatment for older adults depends on professionals' ability to communicate effectively with them. Many older persons have difficulty sensing and discriminating stimuli from the environment because of a decline in the function of the sensory organs, so they may have a harder time attending to and maintaining a conversation. Some aging-related changes and medical conditions that make communication challenging include the following:

- Sensory loss (e.g., hearing, vision)
- Neurological impairment (e.g., stroke, aphasia)
- Cognitive changes (e.g., memory loss)
- Mood disorders (e.g., depression, anxiety)
- Effects of medication
- Poorly fitted dentures

Successful communication with older adults in a counseling situation is dependent upon the ability to conduct effective interviews. Several techniques[1] are of value for diagnostic and therapeutic communication:

- Older adults should be approached with dignity and respect. Individuals should be addressed by their proper names, such as Ms. Peterson, Dr. Ross, or Mr. Barnes. If the older person prefers to be called by another name, wait for a cue that familiarity is permissible.

- If visiting clients in their home or a long-term care or medical setting, be careful to respect their privacy. Knock on the door before entering their home or room.

- During the interview, sit as near to older adults as possible, and be aware of their difficulty with discriminating sensory stimuli.

- Clarify the purpose of the interview and explain why you are taking notes or recording.

- During the interview, speak clearly and slowly. Simple sentences are the most effective means of communicating with older adults who have hearing or memory loss. Only one question should be asked at a time.

- Balance systematic inquiry into problems with unstructured and undirected periods of conversation during the interview. This permits older adults to state the nature of the problem in their own words as well as to connect past and present.

- Ask open-ended questions that allow for elaboration (e.g., "Tell me about your family" or "What makes you feel sad?").

- Pace the interview so that older adults are given enough time to respond to inquiries and relay their view of the problem.

- Be alert to nonverbal communication. Facial expressions, eye contact, gestures, and posture all provide messages about how older adults are feeling and responding during the interview.

- Use terminology that is easily understood by older clients. Be alert for nonverbal signs of incomprehension, such as squinting, a furrowed brow, or a blank or quizzical expression.

- Use touch to help older adults relax, feel supported, and communicate more effectively. Holding their hand or resting a hand on their arm can be a reassuring form of nonverbal communication. If older adults show discomfort when being touched, respect their feelings.

- If spouses, adult children, or caregivers have come with clients, look for patterns of control and submission. Clients should be encouraged to speak for themselves whenever possible. Social workers should focus eye contact and questions on clients. If a person or family member accompanying the client tries to dominate the conversation, respond by instructing him or her to let the client answer questions. If the other people do not comply, they should be asked to leave the room.

- If a client rambles, consider a tactful interruption. Social workers can ask for clarification, summarize, or ask a new question.

- Encourage reticent clients to speak or elaborate with brief remarks (e.g., "Tell me more"), nods, and periods of silence. Sometimes it is helpful to rephrase or repeat the question.

- Summarize and repeat key points when closing the session. Ask for feedback to assess the client's understanding of what transpired during the session and the plans for follow-up.

Most older adults are realistic about their physical and emotional challenges and want professionals to be honest as well as hopeful. Give clients hope by concentrating on the present and avoiding unrealistic expectations about the future. Potentially harmful responses to client concerns include the following:

- *Denial* (e.g., "You really don't mean that") gives clients the impression that social workers don't take their statements or feelings seriously or that their feelings are not real or appropriate.

- *Judgment* (e.g., "You shouldn't feel that way") indicates a negative reaction to clients' behaviors or expressions of thoughts and feelings.

- *Argument* is a combination of denial and judgment that disputes clients' statements or feelings.

Many older adults accept myths about aging, which may cause those myths to become self-fulfilling prophecies. Common misconceptions about aging that can interfere with counseling are the ideas that older people cannot change or that once they retire or get older they will be depressed. In truth, counseling with older adults is effective, perhaps as much as with clients of other ages. Counseling can address the issues and problems of later life and help restore people to a fulfilling and productive life. Timely interventions can improve functioning and may even be cost-effective in keeping older adults mentally and physically healthy.

Counseling Older Adults

To meet the needs of older clients through counseling, social workers must realize that the roles and functioning of older people vary widely. It is important to view older adults as individuals first. Understanding the client's past life experiences and roles is critical when counseling older adults, specifically clients' roles as workers, family members, neighbors, and friends. Drawing on older adults' life experiences and strengths will help these clients adjust to the challenges they may encounter as a result of the aging process. Several approaches promote successful counseling relationships with older adults:

- *Patience* for the time required for some older adults to respond or complete tasks

- *Teamwork* with family and other providers (shared authority)

- *Capacity to anticipate* older adults' needs and advocate for care

- *Appreciation* for cultural and physiological diversity among older adults

In contrast, social workers should avoid these inappropriate and ineffective styles of interaction that are sometimes used when counseling older adults:

- *Overprotectiveness*: This paternalistic approach assumes that because clients are older, they are unable to do things for themselves. It may also be an attempt by counselors to control the counseling session and may stem from counselors' lack of patience in allowing clients time to complete a task at their own speed.

- *"Anything goes"*: Some counselors accept destructive behaviors in older adults that would be considered unacceptable in young adults (e.g., excessive drinking, verbal abuse).

- *Insensitivity:* This style of interaction is often seen in counselors who do not demonstrate an understanding of aging issues and the need for older clients to remain independent and retain control of their situations. It often stems from a lack of knowledge or training in the aging process.

Multicultural Counseling

As with all client populations, older adults are diverse and do not respond to a one-size-fits-all approach to treatment and practice techniques. The social worker's role is to help older persons function with pride, dignity, and as much independence as possible. Individuals' strengths and coping skills should be identified and utilized. Religious faith, family ties, and a sense of community are often sources of strength for older adults.

Multicultural counseling focuses on understanding not only racial and ethnic minority groups (e.g., African Americans, Asian Americans, Hispanics, Native Americans), but also LGBTQ men and women, people with intellectual or developmental disabilities, and a variety of other populations with special needs. Many mental health providers are still ill-prepared to discuss meaningful topics with older adults of different racial, ethnic, or cultural backgrounds. For example, professionals may struggle to discuss issues surrounding relationships, sexuality, and family with LGBTQ older adults and their loved ones.

Multicultural counseling and psychotherapy challenge the idea that personal problems are exclusively within the individual, instead emphasizing the social and cultural context of human behavior and the relationship between individuals and their environment. Social workers must recognize that many problems reside outside individuals, such as prejudice and discrimination. To provide culturally effective interventions, social workers may need to assume nontraditional roles that may include advocate, change agent, consultant, adviser, and facilitator of indigenous support or healing systems.[2,3]

Psychosocial Intervention Models

Chosen therapeutic techniques should be tailored to older adults' preferences, flexibility, and cognitive ability. Circumstances related to physical mobility or transportation may allow for few or infrequent visits, making trips to the therapist's office difficult. Social workers in geriatric practice often find that it is more convenient for older clients to be seen in out-of-office settings, such as their home or retirement community. The choice of therapeutic intervention for older clients should be based on (1) the client's situation and needs, (2) the client's functional ability, and (3) available resources. Many counseling orientations and treatment approaches are available for older adults.

Ecological Systems Theory

Ecological systems theory sees individuals as integrated members of their communities and the wider society.[4] Systems perspectives are based on the premise that people are in constant interaction with their environment. Individuals move through a series of life transitions that necessitate environmental support and coping skills. Social workers should look holistically at older adults and their environments to develop the most effective care or treatment plan. The ecological framework helps social workers organize information about people and their environments in order to understand how the two are interconnected:

- Presenting problems should be defined in terms of family and community systems as well as the client's culture, ethnicity, and heritage.

- Service planning should consider the full range of options and choices available to the client and his or her family. Service options may include home health services, respite care, support groups, in-home care, and, when necessary, residential care.

Family Systems Theory

A knowledge of family-system dynamics helps in assessing and addressing client issues related to caregiving and family conflicts. Seeing older adults in the context of their informal support systems can help social workers develop an effective service plan and deepen their understanding of the roles clients and family members play within the family system. Social work interventions should be based on older clients' and their families' definitions of problems, goals, needs, and solutions. From a family systems perspective, several concepts can assist the social worker:[5]

- Some families are highly enmeshed, sustaining rather than resolving conflict in an inefficient pattern of preserving solidarity instead of the individual competence of each family member.

- Some families may be close but manage to work out conflict without subverting individuals.

- Certain families may be overprotective, rigid, and prone to avoiding conflict at all costs.

- Family boundaries may be open or closed and yet still be effective in meeting older adults' needs for both support and autonomy. Families with an open boundary system allow outside elements and situations to influence the family system. Families with a closed boundary system are self-contained and isolate members from the outside environment. No family system is completely open or closed.

- Families may have distorted beliefs or false attributions, leading them to be pessimistic or cynical about assistance or the ability to adapt to a difficult situation.

Psychotherapy

Older adults are particularly receptive to short-term, focused forms of psychotherapy that have been recently developed. In fact, older adults who enter psychotherapy may be more willing to follow treatment recommendations, less prone to dropping out of therapy, and more positive toward treatment than other age groups.[6,7] Research has shown that psychotherapy in combination with medication is more effective than single-modality treatment.[8-10] Given the serious consequences of relapse for individuals with mental health disorders, medication monitoring through psychotherapy may be justification for periodic visits, which can be important in helping older adults adhere to their medication regimens.

Table 5.1 describes different types of psychotherapy that may benefit older adults. All forms of psychotherapy have the potential to provide a supportive therapeutic relationship, examine cognitive distortions, address conflict and ambivalence, repair interpersonal or intrapsychic deficits, and restructure defenses.[11]

Table 5.1 Types of Psychotherapy for Older Adults

Therapy	Benefits for Older Adults
Cognitive-behavioral therapy[12]	• Focus on the relationship between thoughts, feelings, and behaviors • Countering misperceptions, mistaken beliefs • Directive, symptom-focused approach • Techniques practiced outside therapy sessions
Life review, reminiscence therapy[13]	• Recall of personal history to master one's present and future • Intervention based on the older adult's strengths
Short-term psychodynamic therapy[14]	• Focus on a problem
Problem-solving therapy[15]	• Focus on change; narrow and pragmatic • Teaching clients how to apply a problem-solving method to develop their own solutions
Supportive therapy[16]	• Maintenance of present level of functioning and control of symptoms
Caregiver counseling[17]	• Focus on the caregiver role • Combining elements of cognitive-behavioral and interpersonal therapy
Bereavement therapy[18]	• Restructuring client's experience of the person lost
Validation therapy[19]	• Successful use with persons with dementia • Affirming that irrational speech and behavior occur for a reason • Validating what is said by encouraging and expanding messages to show unconditional regard for the individual
Crisis intervention[20]	• Use when person is dealing with an acute crisis • Seven stages: assessment of safety and lethality, building rapport, identifying problems, addressing feelings, generating alternatives, developing an action plan, and providing follow-up

Reality Orientation

Reality orientation is a cognitive rehabilitation program that became popular in the 1970s.[21] The program originated in the psychiatric hospital setting, where it was developed to orient persons with a moderate to severe degree of confusion, disorientation, and memory loss. Basic information, such as the day of the week; the date, month, and year; and name and location of the person's residence, is reinforced on a continual basis. This program was later implemented in the nursing home setting, where it was thought to be successful in improving and maintaining orientation in persons with memory disorders. All nursing home staff, from the facility's administrator to nursing, dietary, and housekeeping employees, were trained to orient residents.

Although this strategy continues to be used successfully with persons who have mild cognitive impairment, it is no longer considered to be an appropriate approach in working with those individuals in the later stages of dementia.[22] When short-term memory loss becomes acute, it is difficult for the person with dementia to retain the information, and he or she may become frustrated.

Group Counseling

Counseling groups can help older adults handle the developmental tasks and challenges of aging in a way that maintains their integrity and self-respect. Counseling groups for older adults do not need to be homogeneous in terms of age, gender, income, or marital status. Group counseling involves strategies and activities that promote understanding and appreciation of diversity within the group in areas such as culture, ethnicity, race, gender, class, religion, and sexual orientation. However, differences in cognitive impairment, physical disability or frailty, hearing loss, or language will often prevent the development of group cohesion and therapeutic success.

Many counseling groups share some of the same procedures, techniques, and processes. They differ, however, with respect to specific aims, the role of the group leader, group members, and focus. Several types of counseling groups can help older adults:

- *Psychotherapy groups:* Whereas most counseling groups focus on self-awareness, prevention of problems, growth, and development, psychotherapy groups typically focus on remediation, treatment, and personality reconstruction. Some therapy groups are designed to correct emotional and behavioral disorders that impede one's functioning or to remediate in-depth psychological problems. Group members may be struggling with severe emotional problems or deep neurotic conflicts. Many of them may need remedial treatment rather than developmental and preventive counseling. For this reason, psychotherapy groups tend to be longer-term treatments than other kinds of groups.

- *Psychoeducation groups:* These are usually short-term groups that deal with a specific theme or population. Such groups serve several purposes: providing information, sharing common experiences, teaching people to solve problems, offering support, and helping people learn how to create their own support systems outside of the group setting.

- *Self-help groups:* These groups enable people with a common problem or life predicament to create a support system that helps them cope with psychological stress and gives them the incentive to make changes in their lives. The members share their experiences, provide one another with emotional and social support, learn from one another, and offer suggestions to new members. Self-help groups differ from therapy groups in that they focus on a single issue or topic, such as substance abuse, cancer, or caregiving. The group becomes a means of helping people modify their beliefs, attitudes, and feelings about themselves. Many group leaders of self-help groups are not mental health professionals but may be persons who have experienced similar issues.

In addition to being therapeutic for older clients, group counseling can be a powerful source of support for their families and caregivers. As the facilitator of several caregiver counseling groups, I witnessed the healing power of the group process firsthand.

As I began an exercise that I had used many times in caregiver groups, I prepared myself for the group members' reactions and the floodgate of emotions that usually ensued. I handed each person a piece of paper and asked the group members to write answers to the following questions:

1. What are your plans for the rest of today?

2. What are your plans for the rest of the week?

3. What are your plans for the rest of this year?

4. What are your plans for the next 5 years?

5. What are your plans for the future?

I watched as they diligently wrote down their answers, most of them giving the exercise a lot of thought. After about 10 minutes, I asked them to hand in their answers. A chorus of gasps filled the room as the group watched me tear the papers into small pieces.

"I know that you gave these questions a lot of thought when you answered them, just as you have probably given much thought to your hopes and dreams for the future," I explained. "But, when you become a caregiver, you may find that you have to put those plans aside. As John Lennon said, 'Life is what happens to us when we are making other plans.' There is also an old saying that 'what happens to us in life is not as important as how we handle it.' The care recipient, the caregiver, family, and friends are living in a parallel process. Together you are experiencing continual changes, innumerable losses and mortality issues, and all the strong feelings they evoke. These are some of the subtleties of caregiving, and they are often invisible to others."

The exercise helped the group participants, all caring for spouses, partners, parents, and other family members, to begin talking not only about how caregiving was changing their lives, but also about their anger, sadness, and frustration. These were feelings that they had been unable to share with family and friends because admitting to them caused guilt, shame, and oftentimes negative reactions from others. The group was a safe, nonjudgmental place for participants to discuss these emotions with others who had similar feelings about their caregiving situation.

Transference and Countertransference in Counseling and Psychotherapy

Transference is a psychological phenomenon whereby unconscious hopes, fears, and attitudes are evoked in the client by the therapist.[11,23] Transference in older adults evolves out of childhood relationships as well as significant adult relationships but is exacerbated by stress and conflict. Certain transferences occur more frequently in late life as the older adult confronts the loss of goals and ideals, changes in family and close relationships, illness, disability, and mortality. An example of transference is when a client is grieving the death of a spouse or reacting to placement in a nursing home and develops bitter feelings toward the therapist. Recognizing elements of transference that are taking place allows the therapist to work toward a more reality-based relationship with the client.

Lack of experience with older adults makes a therapist more vulnerable to countertransference, in which feelings are evoked in the therapist by the client. A review of therapists' unconscious reactions to the older client suggests several problems that the therapist may encounter:[23]

- The therapist may be influenced by ageist stereotypes, such as beliefs that older adults lack the capacity for change and that working with them is difficult, unappealing, and unproductive.

- Physical morbidity and approaching mortality may overshadow any reward that the therapist might find in the therapy relationship.

- The therapist's unresolved conflicts over dependency, illness, parental rejection, or threatened engulfment may be evoked.

These reactions may lead to unconscious avoidance and distancing in therapy, making empathy difficult. Lost opportunities for the therapist to encourage the client to develop other attachments and activities outside the therapy, failure to terminate after treatment goals are met, and overlong or indulgent visits or phone calls are examples of countertransference phenomena in therapy with older adults.

Termination of Counseling

Social workers should make every attempt to continue relationships with older clients, avoiding transfers and abrupt terminations when possible. Social workers often become important people in the lives of older adults. Older persons may be experiencing multiple losses in their lives and could easily see the termination of a counseling relationship as yet another loss.

Social work interventions can help improve and enrich the later years for older clients. Those of us who have devoted our lives to the care of older adults find satisfaction in relieving their emotional and social challenges. Most importantly, we can help older adults recognize and realize their potential to modify their lives, increase their adaptation and resiliency, and improve their well-being.

CHAPTER NOTES

1. Blazer, D. (1998). *Emotional problems in later life: Intervention strategies for professional caregivers* (2nd ed.). New York: Springer Publishing Company.
2. Atkinson, D.R., Thompson, E.E., & Grant, S.K. (1993). A three-dimensional model for counseling racial/ethnic minorities. *The Counseling Psychologist, 21*(2), 257–277.
3. For further reading on multicultural counseling, see Corey, G. (2016). *Theory and*

practice of group counseling (9th ed.). Boston: Cengage Learning; Atkinson, D.R., Morten, G., & Sue, D.W. (2003). *Counseling American minorities: A cross-cultural perspective* (6th ed.). Boston: McGraw-Hill.

4. Bronfenbrenner, U. (1979). *The ecology of human development: Experiments by nature and design.* Cambridge, MA: Harvard University Press.

5. Minuchin, S., Rosman, B.L., & Baker, L. (1978). *Psychosomatic families: Anorexia in context.* Cambridge, MA: Harvard University Press.

6. Nordhus, H., & Nielsen, G.H. (1999). Brief dynamic psychotherapy with older adults. *Journal of Clinical Psychology, 55*(8), 935–947.

7. Gallagher-Thompson, D., & Thompson, L.W. (1982). Treatment of major depressive disorder in older adult outpatients with brief psychotherapies. *Psychotherapy: Theory, Research & Practice, 19*(4), 482–490.

8. Seligman, M.E. (1995). The effectiveness of psychotherapy: The Consumer Reports study. *American Psychologist, 50*(12), 965–974.

9. Arnow, B.A., & Constantino, M.J. (2003). Effectiveness of psychotherapy and combination treatment for chronic depression. *Journal of Clinical Psychology, 59*(8), 893–905.

10. de Jonghe, F., Kool, S., van Aalst, G., Dekker, J., & Peen, J. (2001). Combining psychotherapy and antidepressants in the treatment of depression. *Journal of Affective Disorders, 64*(2–3), 217–299.

11. Kennedy, G.J. (2000). *Geriatric mental health care.* New York: The Guilford Press.

12. For further reading on cognitive-behavioral therapy, see Laidlaw, K. (2015). *CBT for older people: An introduction.* Washington, DC: SAGE Publications; Gallagher-Thompson, D., & Thompson, L.W. (2010). *Treating late-life depression: A cognitive behavioral therapy approach, therapist guide.* New York: Oxford University Press; Gorenstein, E.E., & Papp, L.A. (2007). Cognitive-behavioral therapy for anxiety in the elderly. *Current Psychiatry Reports, 9*(1), 20–25.

13. For further reading on reminiscence and life review, see Haber, D. (2006). Life review: Implementation, theory, research, and therapy. *International Journal of Aging and Human Development, 63*(2), 153–171; Haight, B.K., & Burnside, I. (1993). Reminiscence and life review: Explaining the differences. *Archives of Psychiatric Nursing, 7*(2), 91–98; Priefer, B.A., & Gambert, S.R. (1984). Reminiscence and life review in the elderly. *Psychiatric Medicine, 2*(1), 91–100; Butler, R.N. (1963). The life review: An interpretation of reminiscence in the aged. *Psychiatry, 26*(1), 65–76.

14. For further reading on short-term psychodynamic psychotherapy, see Morgan, A.C. (2003). Psychodynamic psychotherapy with older adults. *Psychiatric Services, 54*(12), 1592–1594; Anderson, A.A., & Slatkin, S.E. (1999). Intensive short-term dynamic psychotherapy in the elderly. *The American Journal of Geriatric Psychiatry, 7*(4), 13.

15. For further reading on problem-solving therapy, see Simon, S.S., Cordás, T.A., & Bottino, C.M. (2015). Cognitive behavioral therapies in older adults with depression and cognitive deficits: A systematic review. *International Journal of Geriatric Psychiatry, 30*(3), 223–233; Kiosses, D.N., & Alexopoulos, G.S. (2014). Problem-solving therapy in the elderly. *Current Treatment Options in Psychiatry, 1*(1), 15–26.

16. For further reading on supportive therapy, see Alexopoulos, G.S., Raue, P., &

Areán, P. (2003). Problem-solving therapy versus supportive therapy in geriatric major depression with executive dysfunction. *The American Journal of Geriatric Psychiatry, 11*(1), 46–52; Stanley, M.A., Beck, J.G., & DeWitt Glassco, J. (1996). Treatment of generalized anxiety in older adults: A preliminary comparison of cognitive-behavioral and supportive approaches. *Behavior Therapy, 27*(4), 565–581.

17. For further reading on caregiver counseling, see Brodaty, H., Green, A., & Koschera, A. (2003). Meta-analysis of psychosocial interventions for caregivers of people with dementia. *Journal of the American Geriatrics Society, 51*(5), 657–664; Toner, M.A., & Shadden, B.B. (2002). Counseling challenges: Working with older clients and caregivers. *Contemporary Issues in Communication Science and Disorders, 29,* 68–78; Zarit, S.H., & Zarit, J.M. (1998). *Mental disorders in older adults: Fundamentals of assessment and treatment.* New York: The Guilford Press; Kaplan, M. (1996). *Clinical practice with caregivers of dementia patients.* Bristol, PA: Taylor & Francis.

18. For further reading on bereavement counseling, see Bonifas, R.P. (2018). Grief, loss, and bereavement in older adults: Reactions to death, chronic illness and disability: A learning module for effective social work practice with older adults [PowerPoint presentation]. Retrieved from https://www.cswe.org/Centers-Initiatives/CSWE -Gero-Ed-Center/Initiatives/Past-Programs/MAC-Project/Gero-Innovations -Grant/Arizona-State-University/Grief,-Loss-Bereavement.aspx; Caserta, M.S., & Lund, D.A. (1992). Bereaved older adults who seek early professional help. *Death Studies, 16*(1), 17–30; DeBor, L., Gallagher, D., & Lesher, E. (1983). Group counseling with bereaving elderly. *Journal of Clinical Gerontology, 1*(3), 81–90.

19. Feil, N., & de Klerk-Rubin, V. (2012). *The validation breakthrough: Simple techniques for communicating with people with Alzheimer's and other dementias.* Baltimore: Health Professions Press.

20. For further reading on crisis intervention, see Jungers, C.M., & Slagel, L. (2009). Crisis model for older adults: Special considerations for an aging population. *AdultSpan Journal, 8*(2), 92–101; Iscoe, I., & Duffy, M. (2003). Crisis intervention in older adulthood. In T.P. Gullotta (Ed.), *Encyclopedia of primary prevention and health promotion.* Boston: Springer Publishing Company, 372-377.

21. For further reading on reality orientation, see Chiu, H.Y., Chen, P.Y., Chen, Y.T., & Huang, H.C. (2018). Reality orientation therapy benefits cognition in older people with dementia: A meta-analysis. *International Journal of Nursing Studies, 86,* 20–28; Patton, D. (2006). Reality orientation: Its use and effectiveness within older person mental health care. *Journal of Clinical Nursing, 15*(11), 1440–1449; Drummond, L., Kirchhoff, L., & Scarbrough, D.R. (1978). A practical guide to reality orientation: A treatment approach for confusion and disorientation. *The Gerontologist, 18*(6), 568–573; Taulbee, L.R., & Folsom, J.C. (1966). Reality orientation for geriatric patients. *Hospital & Community Psychiatry, 17*(5), 133–135.

22. Dietch, J.T., Hewett, L.J., & Jones, S. (1989). Adverse effects of reality orientation. *Journal of the American Geriatrics Society, 37*(10), 974–976.

23. Lazarus, L.W., & Sadavoy, J. (1996). Individual psychotherapy. In J. Sadavoy, L.W. Lazarus, L. Jarvik, & G.T. Grossberg (Eds.), *Comprehensive review of geriatric psychiatry-II* (2nd ed.) (pp. 819–850). Washington, DC: American Psychiatric Press.

SECTION III

Issues and Challenges in Late Life

The needs of older adults, like those of any population group, are diverse and complex. These needs may range from mental health and family counseling services, housing, and recreation and wellness programs to the evolving continuum of long-term care. Social workers have a special role to play in the care of older adults because they do not consider just one aspect of care but develop plans to meet the multivariate needs of older adults and their families. Social work is uniquely focused on the whole person, addressing medical and mental healthcare, social needs, and other aspects of the person's welfare. Just as health is not only the absence of disease, successful aging is not just the absence of psychosocial problems. Rather, it is how the individual copes with the challenges of late life. The following chapters address the issues that many individuals experience as they age and discuss recommendations for assessment, strategies, and therapeutic interventions based on an understanding of cultural and social diversity.

Mental Health

An estimated 20% of people aged 55 and older experience some type of mental health concern.[1] However, it is unlikely that an individual will experience the initial onset of a serious mental health disorder (e.g., schizophrenia) in old age. Many older adults experience mental health challenges and symptoms of mental disturbance. Although not usually serious enough to be diagnosed as illnesses, these symptoms may interfere with normal functioning and often diminish quality of life.

There are multiple risk factors for mental health problems in later life. As we age, we encounter many challenges that threaten our self-image and independence. Older adults may experience significant loss of capacities and a decline in functional abilities as a result of reduced mobility, chronic pain, frailty, or other health problems. In addition, older adults are more likely to experience traumatic events or stressors, such as bereavement or a decrease in socioeconomic status after retirement. These stressors can result in isolation, loneliness, and psychological distress. In addition to affecting a person's mental health, stress that becomes excessive or lasts for a long time can also affect physical health, exacerbating medical conditions such as stroke, diabetes, and heart disease. Possible triggers for mental health problems in older adults include the following:

- Decline in physical abilities and health

- Chronic pain

- Changes in family and professional roles, such as the "empty nest" and retirement

- Decrease in financial independence

- Moving to a new living environment

- Loss of mobility and transportation

- Increased caregiving demands (e.g., taking care of an ill spouse or another family member)

- Loss of spouse, family members, and friends to death or relocation

- Certain medications

- Substance abuse

When talking with a healthcare provider, older adults are less likely to disclose symptoms related to mental health problems than they are physical symptoms. This may be because some individuals fail to recognize that the symptoms are signs of a mental health disorder. In other cases, persons do not disclose symptoms because of the stigma associated with mental health problems. However, older adults are increasingly seeking professional mental health services for help with their problems. Some individuals may have been in treatment earlier in their lives and may not have experienced the same level of stigma that was felt by previous generations.

Social workers who serve older adults can identify signs of mental health issues in their clients and their clients' family members. Common indicators of mental health problems include the following:

- A marked change in appetite, energy level, and/or mood

- Persistent hopelessness, sadness, or suicidal thoughts

- A flat affect (i.e., lack of emotional response or expression)

- A change in sleeping habits (e.g., trouble falling or staying asleep; sleeping too much)

- A dependence on drugs or alcohol

- Restlessness or difficulty concentrating

- Increased feelings of stress or anxiety

- Increased anger, agitation, and/or aggressiveness

- Obsessive-compulsive behavioral tendencies or thoughts

- Thoughts or behaviors that negatively affect relationships

- Persistent digestive problems, pain, or headaches unexplained by medical conditions

- Difficulty managing finances or routine tasks

Outside of hospitals or long-term care settings, approximately one-third of older adults receive outpatient mental health treatment from a family physician, and another third do not receive any treatment. Only a small number of older adults ever receive treatment from a mental health professional.[2]

Common Mental Health Issues in Older Adults

Common mental health disorders or symptoms experienced by older adults can be treated with medication, nonpharmacological interventions, or a combination of the two. The most common reasons for prescribing psychiatric medication to an older adult and the class of medications used for treatment include

- Depression (antidepressants)

- Anxiety, rumination, fears and phobias (anxiolytics)

- Agitation (antipsychotics, mood stabilizers)

- Sleep disorders (hypnotics)

- Psychotic thinking, including delusions of others' malevolent intent (antipsychotics)

The Diagnostic and Statistical Manual of Mental Disorders, 5th Edition (DSM-5), used by clinicians and researchers to diagnose and classify mental disorders, is the accepted source to facilitate an objective assessment of symptom presentations in a variety of clinical settings.[3] The mental disorders discussed in this chapter are recognized in the DSM-5.

Many older adults in long-term care have mental disorders, most commonly depression, agitation, or a combination of several conditions. The number of medications they receive is substantially higher than the number of medications taken by older adults living in the community.[4] Not all older adults with mental health symptoms or disorders should be treated with medication. Whenever possible, medications should not be the first intervention used if there are effective alternative treatments. Some nonpharmacological techniques that can be used alone or in conjunction with medication include

- Individual or group psychotherapy provided by a licensed mental health professional

- Participation in a support group that consists of other older adults with similar problems

- Exercise and physical activity

- Participation in creative or educational activities

- Community service and volunteer activities

Loneliness

Loneliness has been identified as a common problem for older adults, reported by as many as 31% globally and 19% in the United States.[5,6] Linked to psychological and physiological health problems, loneliness is a major predictor of depressive symptoms, functional decline, and mortality in older adults. Negative emotional responses to loneliness, such as worry, anger, fear, and sadness, are common.

The social stigma of loneliness often results in self-isolation and decreased community involvement. Older adults at increased risk for loneliness include individuals who are single; live alone; or have lower incomes, low educational levels, a poor self-report of health, chronic illnesses, or functional impairments (e.g., gross and fine motor impairments). Poor health outcomes associated with loneliness include less physical activity, more tobacco use, a greater number of chronic illnesses, higher depression scores, and a higher-than-average number of nursing-home stays.[7] The negative health and psychosocial effects of loneliness suggest that screening for loneliness should be included as part of a geriatric assessment.

Once loneliness has been recognized, it is important to discuss this issue with the individual. Loneliness Intervention using Story Theory to Enhance Nursing-sensitive outcomes (LISTEN)[1] is one therapeutic intervention model being used to reduce the social stigma associated with loneliness and to help older adults cope with the challenges of loneliness. The core topics of LISTEN include sense of belonging over the life course, past and current relationships, community involvement, the meaning of loneliness, and coping with loneliness. Discussing these topics helps people identify what is important to them in their personal experience of loneliness, derive a personal meaning of loneliness and belonging, sort out positive and negative personal relationships, identify ways of participating in communities, accept the personal challenges of loneliness, and develop potential new ways of coping with loneliness.

Depression

Depression, a type of mood disorder, is the most prevalent mental health problem among older adults.[1] Although the rate of older adults with depressive symptoms tends to increase with age, the pervasive and debilitating illness of major depressive disorder is not an inevitable part of aging. The sadness, sense of loss, and loss of purpose that often occur in late life are not necessarily evidence of clinical depression.

The term "late-onset depression" refers to a depression that occurs for the first time after age 65. Older adults who have had prior depression (called early-onset depression) do not respond to antidepressant medications as well as those people who experience depression for the first time in late life and often need specialized treatment by a geriatric psychiatrist.

Although women are more likely to be affected by depression than men, depression is especially common in older men. Older men have the highest suicide rate of any age group, with a rate of 45.23 suicides per 100,000 for individuals 85 and older compared to an overall rate of 11.01 suicides per 100,000 for all ages.[8] The risk of suicide is especially high in recently bereaved older men who have no family or social support.

Common Causes of Late-Life Depression.   The prevalence of significant depressive symptoms increases in older adults who have chronic medical disorders and disabilities. Arthritis, heart disease, and cancer are some of the medical conditions that are frequently associated with depression in late life. Some older adults experiencing physical symptoms may be unaware of depressive symptoms or unable to express their feelings. Suppressed or painful emotions may be more difficult to express or be seen as less acceptable than physical symptoms. When physical or somatic symptoms take the forefront in an adult experiencing depression, this condition is sometimes identified as masked depression.

Depression is also common in older adults with neurological disorders. Depressive symptoms are often present in persons with dementia of the Alzheimer's type, with the degree of symptomatology ranging from mild depression to the severe emotional lability that accompanies the late stages of the disease. Because depression and physical illness often coexist, a medical examination is an essential early part of any psychiatric diagnostic evaluation. Laboratory tests should also be performed to identify any hidden metabolic or endocrine disorders that can be treated.

It is important to determine whether an older adult has a clinical depressive disorder or is experiencing a fluctuation in mood. Clinical depression encompasses a range of moods and disturbed affect and is usually divided into three subtypes: major depressive disorder, the most serious form; persistent depressive disorder (i.e., dysthymia), a chronic but less severe state of depression usually mixed with anxiety; and minor or subsyndromal depression, in which depressive symptoms are persistent but not severe.[9]

The story of Donna, my last client as a practicing social worker, is an example of how depression can impact a person's quality of life and how it can be addressed by placing the client's needs and interests at the forefront.

I tried to call Donna several times, but there was no answer, and she did not have voicemail. It had been a month since my last visit. Donna had been recovering from a fall in her apartment and had complained about her doctor's insistence that she have a home health aide and physical therapy. At the age of 97, she was still fiercely independent and resented having people tell her what to do. She had no family nearby, so I contacted the office at the retirement community where she lived. They told me that Donna had passed away suddenly 2 weeks ago. There was no funeral service, at her request.

I first met Donna 7 years earlier, when I received a referral from the retirement community activity coordinator. Donna had inquired about getting some counseling, and I was seeing several clients in her building at the time. When I arrived for my first home visit, Donna told me that her physician said that she needed to "talk to someone." She told me that she was a widow and had two children who lived at a distance (one in another country). She admitted to feeling depressed about her recent falls but said that her health continued to be good, although she was finding it difficult to walk distances. She agreed to counseling, and when I arrived the following week, she handed me the following note:

> You said I sound depressed; I countered with frustration. Instead of facing each new day with joy at still being here and alive, I find myself not at all happy to be alive. Most of the freedom and independence I thoroughly enjoyed after my husband died 7 years ago have dreadfully diminished.
>
> The lack of balance gets worse, and my fear of falling gets more intense. My lack of hearing has shadowed me since I was a child, but I did function, whereas now I am clinging to a small amount of sound and fearing it will get even worse. When I was released from my bad marriage, I traveled extensively. With my car, I could do errands as the need arose. Now I no longer have this luxury.
>
> As I face each day, I am frustrated. I have the use of the community's bus and am transported to many of my needs, plus outings on occasion. Occasionally I have had a driver. But these activities need planning, and they are not always what I would have liked. Basically, I have nothing to look forward to. My social life is practically nil, since most people won't or don't make the effort to speak with me in a way that I can handle.
>
> My greatest fear is of the future. What if. . . I cannot do what little I can do for myself now? I am fiercely independent as far as it goes. I shudder to anticipate what my life can become. That's why I need to talk it out with you.

Over the next 3 years, Donna and I worked together to brighten her mood, cope with her disabilities, and find quality in her life. We identified her strengths—she was very proud of her children and grandchildren, was a wonderful artist, and took great pride in her philanthropic activities in the community. With the help of medication, she was able to begin the task of finding ways to experience a better quality of life through her remaining years.

Because Donna was frustrated that her hearing loss made it difficult to communicate with family and friends, we enlisted the help of a computer technician to set up email and Skype capabilities on her computer. She was interested in learning more about her family, many members of whom were Holocaust survivors, and her roots in New York City. I introduced her to genealogy websites and the archives at the New York Public Library. To increase her social contact with other residents in the retirement community, she offered to work on the community newsletter and enrolled in an art class. A companion aide from a home health agency was scheduled to come once a week to take her to lunch, visit museums, and shop. Donna was happy with her progress and decided that we could decrease our sessions to once a month, then gradually to every 3 months.

On my last visit, Donna could hardly wait to tell me what she had been up to lately. "For so long, I have wanted to go back to New York City one last time, but I never had the courage to do so. But last month, I decided to do it, and I booked a flight, made hotel reservations, and got tickets for several shows. I arrived in New York and took a cab to my hotel. My biggest disappointment was that the bar was closed when I arrived at the hotel. For the next 4 days, I walked the city streets with my walker and went to a show each night. I was alone, but I had a wonderful time. I am very proud of myself right now that I was able to accomplish my goal of returning to New York. I know that I will never do it again, but that's okay."

Depression and Bipolar Disorder.   A depression that alternates with states of elated mood, irritability, and excessive activity is considered a bipolar disorder, previously referred to as manic-depressive disorder. Although it is common for bipolar disorder to continue into late life, it is rare for the onset of the disorder to occur in older adults. Depression associated with bipolar illness may gradually or suddenly change into a manic state. In older adults with bipolar disorder, changes in mood become more pronounced as the individual ages, with the severity of each mood state increasing over time. A manic or hypomanic episode later in life presents differently than mania in younger persons. In general, older individuals experiencing mania become more irritable and angrier (dysphoric mania) and less elated and euphoric. It is also not unusual to see paranoia or delusions that others intend to inflict harm. Since antidepressant medication may accelerate mania in bipolar illness, it is important to be aware of a history of prior manias. Indicators of a prior bipolar episode include periods of the following:

- Unusual exuberance

- Loud, rapid, and rambling speech

- Irresponsible money spending

- A notable decrease in need for sleep

- Unusually increased interest in sex

- Elation, euphoria, or grandiosity

- Irritability and unusually short-tempered behavior

Recognizing Symptoms of Depression.   A depressive disorder in older adults is usually easy to recognize. Complaints of little appetite, difficulty sleeping, and loss of interest in usual activities are common. The individual appears listless, withdrawn, and apathetic. Some older adults with depression talk about their unhappiness and express their pain frequently, whereas others seem resigned to quietly living out the rest of their lives feeling sad or hopeless. Compared with younger persons, older persons with depression demonstrate fewer symptoms of guilt and self-reproach and more disturbances in patterns of sleep, appetite, and energy levels.[3]

It is important to ask an older adult with depression about suicidal thoughts. There is a mistaken belief that asking about suicidal thoughts may plant the idea of self-harm and increase the risk of suicide, but the opposite is true. Asking about suicide diminishes the sense of isolation that older adults with depression often feel and may actually reduce the risk. Prior suicide attempts increase the risk of suicide, as does the suicide of a family member or friend. Some individuals may view suicidal thoughts as a shameful sign of their failure to cope with life's problems and should be reassured that these thoughts are symptoms of a treatable illness.

When responding to an older adult who is preoccupied with suicidal thoughts, has attempted suicide in the past, or is currently feeling suicidal, social workers should observe these guidelines:

- Specific plans for completing suicide constitute a very high risk, but the absence of plans does not necessarily mean there is no immediate risk of harm. Suicidal thinking should always be taken seriously.

- Unless the person can be continually monitored for an entire 24-hour period, hospitalization should be considered.

- Any medication that could cause a lethal overdose must be supervised.

- Any potential weapons must be removed from the person's environment.

- The risk of suicide does not decrease when the individual begins taking antidepressant medication. During the early period of anti-depressant treatment, the risk of suicide may increase.

Psychotic Depression.   A severe form of late-life depression is charac-terized by delusional thinking. Also referred to as psychotic depression, the diagnosis of delusional depression is made when there are signs of a major depressive disorder in addition to delusions. The types and exam-ples of delusions that are associated with late-life depression include

- Nihilistic delusions ("I'm hopeless.")

- Somatic delusions ("I have cancer and no one is telling me.")

- Paranoid delusions ("I am being watched by the government.")

Because older adults with psychotic depression usually deny the illness, attributing all symptoms to a delusional belief, they often refuse or do not follow treatment. Life-threatening states of exhaustion, weight loss, electrolyte imbalance, pneumonia, and cardiac arrhythmias may require hospitalization in older adults with psychotic depression.

Treating Late-Life Depression.   Concern, empathy, and supportive lis-tening are important in forming therapeutic relationships with older adults. Social workers should neither patronize clients nor minimize their suffering, but they should encourage older adults to talk openly about their recent losses, suicidal thoughts, and painful feelings in an atmosphere of mutual trust and acceptance. Some older adults may be unable to benefit from psychotherapy until their depression has improved using antidepressant medication. Their lack of motivation and physical or mental energy may prevent them from making appointments and discussing their emotional issues, making it dif-ficult for them to benefit from counseling sessions. Other older individuals who are not candidates for psychotherapy are those in advanced stages of dementia or those with delusions or other forms of psychotic thinking.

In cases involving serious late-life depression, especially depression that includes delusions, the most effective treatment may be electroconvulsive therapy (ECT). In its earlier years as an antidepressant treatment, ECT was controversial because of the administration procedure and its side effects. Modern ECT is now regarded as a safe, effective, and medically sophisticated treatment with well-described standards and procedures.[10] ECT is especially helpful for an older, frail patient whose life may be at risk from severe depressive symptoms. A series of ECT treatments is usually necessary, eventually causing the delusions to disappear. Side effects of ECT include mild, short-term memory loss surrounding recent events that occurred before and during the period of treatment.

It is important to note that most cases of depression in older adults can be successfully treated. Recovery from depression takes time, with several weeks or months of treatment necessary before improvement occurs. Early signs of response to treatment include improved sleep followed by increased attention to grooming and appearance, which may have been neglected during the depressive episode. The case story of Joyce demonstrates successful treatment of depression in an older adult using cognitive behavioral therapy and medication.

Joyce was a 71-year-old retired college professor who came to therapy to address unresolved bereavement issues. She had recently experienced the deaths of her sister-in-law and her sister, for whom she had been a caregiver. She had also been the primary caregiver for her husband, who had died 7 years before.

At the initial interview, Joyce showed signs of self-neglect in her appearance, specifically in her grooming and clothing. She described vegetative symptoms, such as a loss of interest in her usual activities, poor appetite, low energy, and a marked decrease in her ability to carry out instrumental activities of daily living. She also reported episodes of anxiety and a sometimes overwhelming fear of developing Alzheimer's disease based on her family history (sister, mother). Based on my evaluation of Joyce's presenting complaints, acute and chronic stressors, and degree of functional impairment, she was diagnosed as having (1) depressive disorder and (2) unresolved grief and bereavement.

Joyce began weekly therapy sessions with the goals of resolving the debilitating feelings surrounding her losses, decreasing her depression

Table 6.1   Joyce's Treatment Plan

Behaviors to be Changed	Interventions	Indicators of Improvement
1. Feeling sad most of the time, loss of interest in activities, fatigue (loss of energy)	1(a). M.D. referral for anti-depressant 1(b). Set tasks and goals, reassess vegetative symptoms (affect, poor grooming, loss of appetite)	1(a). Improve daily function 1(b). Reduce vegetative symptoms 1(c). Identify and resolve causes of depression
2. Unresolved bereavement of death of sister and sister-in-law and feelings of guilt about caregiving efforts	2(a). Explore current negative grief-related symptoms 2(b). Verbalize bereavement tasks 2(c). Keep journal of symptoms, feelings, and triggers	2(a). Resolve debilitating feelings surrounding losses 2(b). Develop plan for life, renewing old relationships and establishing role in family.

and anxiety, and improving her level of functioning and social contact. It became obvious in the first 2 weeks of therapy that Joyce's depressed mood was preventing her from actively participating in working toward her goals. It was suggested that an antidepressant medication be considered in the treatment of her depressive symptoms. Following a phone consultation with her physician, she began taking sertraline. She experienced adverse reactions to this medication and was then switched to venlafaxine, which she took with good results. As her medication took effect, elevating Joyce's mood and enabling her to begin work on her treatment goals, the treatment plan in Table 6.1 was developed.

Before starting therapy, Joyce had stopped performing the daily tasks necessary to maintain good hygiene, nutrition, and her home environment, as well as her family and social contacts. At her first office visit, Joyce showed signs of self-neglect, her hair matted, her face devoid of the makeup she usually enjoyed wearing, and her clothing disheveled and ill-fitting. A petite woman, she was underweight and seemed to disappear into the cushions of the sofa. Speaking in a soft voice with little affect, she told me that she had been a college professor and retired several years ago to take care of first her husband, then her sister, who was diagnosed with Alzheimer's disease. In the 6 months since her sister's death, Joyce had sunk into a deep depression. She reported that she had no energy or motivation to continue her daily activities or to maintain her social contacts. She was no longer brushing her teeth, preparing meals, or opening her mail and email.

We used a genogram and life review to gather information about her family and her life story. From these tools, I learned that Joyce had experienced significant loss in her childhood in addition to the recent deaths of her husband, sister-in-law, and sister. Her father had died by suicide when she was 9 years old, and her mother assumed the bereavement role for the rest of her life. Cognitive behavioral therapy was used to identify negative thoughts and feelings and to set small, short-term goals to improve Joyce's everyday functioning. The following excerpt is from a written assignment that was designed to help Joyce record and focus on her feelings:

> *Mary instructed me to get in touch with my feelings. Now, I have no idea how to go about this task, and I'm rather anxious. But I've decided to try to write down my feelings at the same time each day:*
>
> > *Thursday: I'm smiling and frowning, wondering where to start. I focus. I feel satisfied, pleased that the day has gone well. I accomplished a few things— shopping, lunching, appointment with Mary, other errands. Feel tension in shoulders. Why? I'm worried about my health—short and long-term. Must stop smoking, start daily walks, perhaps more yoga.*
> >
> > *Friday: Focused . . . on my sister. I feel sad that she's no longer a part of my life. I feel sad that I didn't do more, do things differently. But why was she so stubborn about seeking real medical help or making alternate living arrangements? I acknowledge this: that I felt left out of my family, so I decided to take monthly trips. It was for me, not [my sister]. I'm ashamed. I also felt envious, most of my life—my sister was so pretty, so settled.*

We also worked on identifying weekly tasks for Joyce to complete that could help improve her depression. One by one, Joyce instituted these changes and began the process of reconnecting with herself and with her family and friends. One of the important changes she made was nutritional. Before therapy, Joyce's daily food intake consisted of a small container of yogurt and coffee. Six months into therapy, she had achieved her goal of preparing and eating regular meals. She began by buying single portions of prepared meals, and by the end of therapy, she was not only cooking her meals, but also had remodeled her kitchen and installed bright-red cabinets.

After 6 months of therapy and medication, Joyce began to show considerable improvement in mood, motivation, and functional activity. The specific goals that she had set at the beginning of therapy continued to be reviewed and revised, and several of them had been accomplished. Her therapy sessions were reduced to every 3 weeks, and her medication dose was also reduced.

The woman who came into my office on the final day of therapy was dressed smartly, her gray hair pulled back from her face. She wore large hoop earrings and a silver necklace around her neck. She had recently returned to her church to teach a Bible study course and had signed up to take a watercolor painting class. She was excited to tell me about the trip to California that she was taking to reconnect with her family. Most importantly, she said that she felt an increased satisfaction with life.

Anxiety Disorders

Anxiety, like depression, is one of the most prevalent mental health problems among older adults. Almost half of older adults who are diagnosed with major depression also suffer from anxiety. As a person ages, there are many reasons why he or she may experience anxiety. Multiple losses that include the death of family members and friends and the loss of health and independence are common causes of anxiety in older adults. Anxiety is clinically defined as extreme worry that interferes with normal functioning and quality of life, and in late life, it is almost always accompanied by depression.

In addition to experiencing emotional symptoms of anxiety, such as apprehension, tension, or fear of the future, older adults may also exhibit physical (somatic) symptoms that may present as headaches, pressure in the chest, heart palpitations, difficulty falling asleep, and gastrointestinal discomforts. Because many older adults are more comfortable seeking help for physical complaints than emotional problems, they are more likely to go to their primary physician than a mental health professional. In fact, an older person with anxiety may become obsessed with his or her health, making frequent visits to physicians. Risk factors that are linked to anxiety in older adults include the following:

- Chronic obstructive pulmonary disease (COPD), certain cardiovascular diseases, diabetes, thyroid disease, and related chronic conditions

- Medication side effects
- Abuse of alcohol or drugs
- Physical limitations that affect daily functioning
- Stressful events, such as widowhood or a traumatic experience[3]

Generalized anxiety disorder (GAD) is the diagnostic term used to describe symptoms of anxiety that persist over a period of several weeks and interfere with everyday functioning. These symptoms can get progressively worse with time and eventually interfere with socialization and day-to-day activities. Older adults with GAD tend to become more withdrawn and reclusive. The following symptoms may be experienced by older adults with GAD:

- Excessive, uncontrollable worry or anxiety
- Nervousness or restlessness
- Low energy or chronic fatigue
- Frequent feelings of irritation or agitation

Other anxiety disorders and their associated symptoms include the following:

- *Panic disorder*: a disorder characterized by panic attacks or sudden feelings of extreme apprehension or terror. Signs of a panic attack can include terror; fear of losing control or dying; and physical symptoms such as chest pain, difficulty breathing, and profuse sweating.

- *Phobic disorder*: an intense, specific fear or phobia often accompanied by anxiety and panic. The most common phobias include fear of snakes, insects, heights, enclosed spaces, and large crowds of people. Some older adults have a phobia of being alone or leaving their home. One of the more severe phobias is agoraphobia, the fear of being in places or situations from which escape would be difficult or embarrassing. Older persons suffering from panic and agoraphobia usually restrict travel and often require another person to accompany them when away from home.

- *Post-traumatic stress disorder (PTSD)*: a disorder that usually manifests following a traumatic event that threatens a person's safety or survival. PTSD is characterized by a variable group of symptoms that may include anxiety, interrupted sleep, heart palpitations, sweating, headaches, extreme apprehension, and flashbacks to the traumatic event.

- *Obsessive-compulsive disorder* (OCD): a condition involving extreme anxiety, obsessions, and compulsions. Symptoms of OCD include excessive rumination, repetitive thoughts, and obsessive fears, along with compulsive rituals or behaviors to alleviate the anxiety. Compulsions can take a variety of forms, such as excessive hand-washing or checking of doors, locks, and stoves. Obsessions and compulsions are often accompanied by persistent thoughts of guilt, anger, or low self-esteem. This disorder usually appears in early life and can worsen as the person ages.

When deciding on treatment for an older adult with symptoms of an anxiety disorder, it is important to consider that the symptoms might be caused or exacerbated by medication or be related to a physical illness. A review of the individual's medical report and consultation with his or her physician should take place before beginning treatment. Various approaches and treatments, including medication, psychotherapy, or a combination of both, can be used to address anxiety disorders in older adults.

Bipolar Disorder

The onset of bipolar disorder is typically seen in younger adults, but this illness is frequently misdiagnosed in older adults because bipolar symptoms and behaviors are often misattributed to conditions related to the aging process. Unlike the classic signs exhibited in younger people who are in the manic phase of bipolar disorder, such as high energy and risky behavior, older adults experiencing mania are more likely to become agitated or irritable. Other symptoms in older adults with bipolar disorder may include confusion; hyperactivity; psychosis; or cognitive issues such as memory problems, loss of judgment, and loss of perception. Because the symptoms associated with bipolar disorder may also be caused by the effects of medication or illness, the individual should be diagnosed by a physician to determine the cause of any symptoms and the best options for treatment.

Sleep Disorders

Normal patterns of sleep often change as people age. Although an older adult may spend more time in bed, he or she may actually spend less time sleeping. Falling asleep becomes increasingly difficult; sleep is interrupted by frequent awakenings; and many older adults find that they are fully awake by early morning. This lack of restorative, restful sleep results in a feeling of being tired throughout the day. Some of these sleep changes are caused, in part, by an age-related alteration in monoamine neurotransmission and a decrease in melatonin, the primary hormone that regulates normal sleep cycles.

In addition to age-associated sleep disruption, physical and medical ailments that cause pain and difficulty with breathing are frequent causes of interrupted sleep. Sleep apnea, characterized by struggling to breathe and excessive snoring, not only disturbs sleep, but also can present a serious threat to health. A review of medications can help identify if the person's difficulty sleeping is drug-related. Beta blockers, stimulants, nonprescription decongestants, and appetite suppressants are all drugs that may disrupt sleep and cause daytime drowsiness. Anxiety and depression can also cause sleep disturbance in older adults. Without adequate treatment, the daytime drowsiness and fatigue that result from a lack of sleep can increase anxiety and depression.

Along with treating underlying medical and emotional conditions and decreasing or eliminating any medications that disrupt sleep, short-term use of benzodiazepines may be helpful for some older adults experiencing sleep disturbance. Careful monitoring of the use of benzodiazepines is important because of the risk of dependence and the increased sensitivity to side effects that can occur with these drugs as a person ages. Long-term use of benzodiazepines has been shown to increase daytime drowsiness, falls, automobile accidents, and memory impairments.

Delusional Disorder

Frequently referred to as paranoia, a delusional disorder is most often seen in late life and can cause agitation and disruptive behavior when in a severe form. In addition to being diagnosed as a psychotic disorder, delusions may also be part of a schizophrenic process (e.g., paranoid schizophrenia) or a type of dementia. Examples of common, recurrent delusional themes are that the person's money or items have been stolen or that the person's spouse or partner is having an affair. It is sometimes the case that either some or all of the accusations are based in fact, so the person's concerns should still be validated and the allegations investigated.

Delirium

Delirium initially manifests as fluctuations in consciousness accompanied by confusion, disorientation, and memory impairment. Additional behaviors often include paranoid thinking as well as visual and tactile hallucinations. In older adults, delirium is usually a result of the onset or worsening of a medical condition or a reaction to medication. Common causes of delirium include

- Anticholinergic medications
- Infections, especially urinary tract and respiratory infections
- Dehydration or electrolyte imbalance
- Postoperative reaction to anesthesia
- Congestive heart failure

Because the behaviors seen in a person with delirium may resemble those of dementia, it is important to determine if the individual has any of these health conditions or contributing factors when making a diagnosis. Other factors to consider include the timing of the onset of symptoms and prior history of cognitive status.

Mental Health Assessment, Intervention, and Promotion

It is often difficult to distinguish between mental health and cognitive disorders in older adults. Several assessment tools have proven to be effective in assessing mental health disorders in older persons (see Table 6.2).[11]

Prompt recognition and treatment of mental disorders in older adults is essential to improving their lives and the lives of their family members and caregivers. Helpful interventions include

- Early detection and diagnosis
- Optimizing mental and physical health, functional ability, and quality of life
- Identifying and treating accompanying physical illness
- Counseling therapy to manage stress and maximize social and psychological functioning
- Providing support to families and caregivers

Mental health promotion for older adults involves creating living conditions and environments that support their well-being and enable them to lead healthy lives. Examples of strategies to promote mental health include

- Providing security and freedom to make choices
- Social support for older adults and their caregivers

Table 6.2 Mental Health Assessment Tools

Assessment	Description
The Brief Psychiatric Rating Scale (BPSR)	Administered by a trained interviewer, the BPSR takes about 20 minutes to complete. Following interviews with the individual and a caregiver, scales are drawn to measure cognitive impairment, depression, stroke, and behavioral changes.
Cambridge Mental Disorders of the Elderly Examination (CAMDEX)	The CAMDEX is a more comprehensive assessment that includes eight sections used to diagnose depression, delirium, anxiety, paranoia, and other mental health disorders.
The Geriatric Depression Scale (GDS)	The GDS is a self-reporting scale with 30 yes/no questions. There is a 12-question version that is more commonly used.
The Cornell Scale	The Cornell Scale was specifically designed to identify signs of depression in persons with dementia. Administered by a clinician, the scale is based on interviews with both the older adult and a caregiver.
The Geriatric Mental State Schedule (GMSS)	The GMSS is used to measure the mental health state of older adults in different settings, most often in the community. It is a 45-minute survey administered on a laptop computer.
The Hamilton Rating Scale for Depression	This observer-rated depression scale is administered by a trained professional and takes 30 minutes to complete.

- Adequate living environments

- Health and social programs, with special attention to vulnerable groups such as minority populations, those with special needs, those who live alone, and those with a chronic or relapsing mental or physical illness

Innovations in the domains of psychosocial health, psychotherapy, and pharmacotherapy have shown that recurrence of depression and anxiety in older adults can be prevented, incidence of new disorders can be reduced, and general mental health can be improved and promoted. Mental health promotion for older adults needs to be given the same priority that we give to the promotion of other healthy-living practices.

CHAPTER NOTES

1. Centers for Disease Control and Prevention & National Association of Chronic Disease Directors. (2008). *The state of mental health and aging in America Issue Brief 1: What do the data tell us?* Atlanta, GA: National Association of Chronic Disease Directors.

2. Krajci, K., Vaill, M., Golden, R. (2019) Mental health and aging. Grantmakers in Aging. Retrieved from https://giaging.org.

3. American Psychiatric Association. (2013) *The diagnostic and statistical manual of mental disorders*, 5th edition. Washington, DC: American Psychiatric Association.

4. Burns, E. & McQuillan, N. (2011) Prescribing in care homes: The role of the geriatrician. *Therapeutic Advances in Chronic Disease*, 2(6), 353-358.

5. Theeke, L.A. (2010). Sociodemographic and health-related risks for loneliness and outcome differences by loneliness status in a sample of U.S. older adults. *Research in Gerontological Nursing, 3*(2), 113-125.

6. For further reading on loneliness and older adults, see Shankar, A., McMunn, A., Demakakos, P., Hamer, M., & Steptoe, A. (2017). Social isolation and loneliness: Prospective associations with functional status in older adults. *Health Psychology, 36*(2), 179-187; Lam, C.L.M., Yu, J., & Lee, T.M.C. (2017). Perceived loneliness and general cognitive status in community-dwelling older adults: The moderating influence of depression. *Neuropsychology, Development, and Cognition. Section B: Aging, Neuropsychology, and Cognition, 24*(5), 471-480, doi: https://doi.org/10.1080/13825585.2016.1226246; Perissinotto, C.M., Stijacic Cenzer, I., & Covinsky, K.E. (2012). Loneliness in older persons: A predictor of functional decline and death. *Archives of Internal Medicine, 172* (14), 1078-1083; Luo, Y., Hawkley, L.C., Waite, L.J., & Cacioppo, J.T. (2012). Loneliness, health, and mortality in old age: A national longitudinal study. *Social Science & Medicine, 74*(6), 907-914.

7. Theeke, L.A. (2018). Clinical news: Elders' loneliness constitutes a health problem. *Today's Geriatric Medicine, 11*(2), 27.

8. Sonnega, A., & Weir, D.R. (2014). Health and retirement study: A public resource for data on aging in America since 1990. *Open Health Data, 2*(1), e7. doi: https://doi.org/10.5334/ohd.am

9. Fiske, A., Wetherall, S.L., Gatz, M. (2009) *Annual Review of Clinical Psychology*, 5, 363-389.

10. Lisanby, S.H. (2007) Electroconvulsive therapy for depression. *New England Journal of Medicine*, 357 (19), 1939-45.

11. A comprehensive overview of geriatric assessment tools can be found in Fulmer, T., & Chernof, B. (Eds.) (2018). *Handbook of geriatric assessment* (5th ed.). Sudbury, MA: Jones & Bartlett Learning; Kane, R.L., & Kane, R.A. (2000). *Assessing older persons: Measures, meaning, and practical applications.* New York: Oxford University Press; Rubenstein, L.Z., Wieland, D., & Bernabei, R. (1995). *Geriatric assessment technology: The state of the art.* New York: Springer Publishing Company.

CHAPTER 7

Mental Competence

KEY POINTS

- Client advocacy involves supporting an older adult's choices about treatment and interventions whenever possible.

- When a client's competence is called into question, the social worker should be guided by the principles of decisional capacity.

- Guardianship is the legal intervention often used to care for and protect older adults who are unable to make financial, personal, legal, or healthcare decisions.

FOR OLDER ADULTS, maintaining personal autonomy and making independent decisions are especially important concerns. Personal autonomy is a fundamental value related to our right to make decisions about our lives, exercise control over where and how we live, decide with whom we have relationships, accept or reject medical and social services, and determine how to spend our money. However, for decisions to have personal or legal significance, the individual must have the capacity to make decisions.

The terms "competence" and "capacity" are often used interchangeably, although there is a significant distinction between the two. Competence refers to a legal status related to an individual's right to make life decisions and engage in a variety of transactions with others. Competence can be determined only by a court with appropriate jurisdiction. Capacity refers not to authoritative judicial determinations, but to the working assessments of a person's cognitive and emotional abilities that are conducted by clinicians.[1,2] Social workers who work with older adults encounter a wide variety of issues related to legal competence and functional capacity.

A person's capacity should never be based solely on advanced age or diagnosis, including a diagnosis of Alzheimer's disease or mental illness. Despite the presence of a condition impacting memory or concentration, the individual may still have the residual functional capacity to make meaningful decisions about his or her life and communicate these decisions either verbally or by nonverbal means.

Dementia

Dementia describes a set of symptoms that may include memory loss and difficulties with thinking, problem-solving, or language. According to the Alzheimer's Association, there are approximately 5.7 million people living with dementia in the United States. Most of these cases affect people over the age of 65, with only 5% of cases reported in younger persons.[3] Alzheimer's disease is the most common type of dementia, followed by vascular dementia, dementia with Lewy bodies (DLB), and frontotemporal dementia.[4] Rarer types of dementia include Creutzfeldt-Jakob disease (CJD), Niemann-Pick disease, progressive supranuclear palsy, and brain tumors.

Alzheimer's Disease

Alzheimer's disease is caused by small, abnormal proteins that build up in the brain to form plaques and tangles. This eventually leads to the death of nerve cells and loss of brain tissue. The clinical hallmark of Alzheimer's disease is loss of episodic memory with preservation of long-term or autobiographical memory. This means that the person will continue to have good recollection of events that occurred many years ago but will have poor memory of recent events. A person with Alzheimer's disease might also develop problems with attention span, orientation (e.g., not knowing the day, getting lost in familiar areas), visuospatial skills (misjudging distances), language (e.g., losing words, repeating questions), concentration, and planning (e.g., preparing a meal, making decisions). As the disease progresses, these problems become more severe. In the later stage of Alzheimer's disease, the person may become less aware of the environment, may be unable to identify family members, and may become increasingly frail.

Vascular Dementia

The second-most-common type of dementia, vascular dementia, occurs when there is atherosclerosis in the brain vasculature, often caused by cerebrovascular disease or a stroke. Vascular dementia can cause problems with memory, thinking, and reasoning.

Dementia with Lewy Bodies (DLB)

Lewy bodies are small deposits of a protein called alpha-synuclein that appear within neuronal cell bodies. As they accumulate within the basal ganglia, they cause movement problems similar to Parkinson's disease. The primary clinical feature of DLB is visual hallucinations. Other symptoms include sleeping problems, urinary incontinence, and autonomic dysfunction. It is important to diagnose DLB because treatment with antipsychotics should be avoided in this type of dementia, as these medications can exacerbate hallucinations and cause dystonic reactions.

Frontotemporal Dementia

Frontotemporal dementia affects the frontal lobe of the brain, causing dysfunction in behavior, personality, emotions, facilitation and inhibition, and problem-solving. The temporal lobe is also involved with remembering the meanings of words and names of objects as well as the recognition of faces and objects. Frontotemporal dementia tends to run in families more often than the other types of dementia, with 10%–15% of people affected having a strong family history of the disease.

Clinical Diagnosis of Dementia

There is no single diagnostic test for dementia. Distinguishing Alzheimer's disease from other dementias can only be accomplished through a full dementia workup. The diagnostic category of "dementia NOS" (dementia not otherwise specified) was used in 92.9% of 21.6 million recent fee-for-service Medicare recipients between 2011 and 2013, suggesting that only 7% of older adults received a full cognitive/functional/behavioral history, physical examination, and diagnostic studies to diagnose their type of dementia.[5]

Guardianship of Older Adults

In most states, any individual with serious mental or physical disabilities who is unable to make decisions regarding financial, personal, legal, or healthcare affairs is eligible for an appointed guardian. Guardianship is the legal intervention frequently used to care for and protect older adults. Guardianship is based on the belief that the state has the right and duty to protect individuals and their property when they are unable to adequately care for themselves. The process to obtain guardianship varies from state to state and sometimes from county to county.

State statutes govern the guardianship process, including the petition for determination of incapacity and the appointment of the guardian. In Florida, for example, there are five types of guardianship:[6]

1. *Permanent guardianship* is the most commonly used type of guardianship. The guardian acts on behalf of the individual (ward) until the court finds the ward no longer incapacitated.

2. *Pre-need guardianship* is established by an individual before and in the event of incapacitation.

3. *Emergency temporary guardianship* is used in situations in which there is imminent danger to an individual and his or her health, mental health, or property. The appointment of an emergency temporary guardian may last up to 60 days.

4. *Voluntary guardianship* is used for an individual who is mentally competent but unable to manage his or her assets. In this case, the individual voluntarily requests a guardian to assume these responsibilities.

5. *Standby guardianship* is when a permanent guardian petitions the court to appoint a standby guardian in the event the permanent guardian dies, is removed, or resigns.

Some older adults with mental impairment have family members who make their decisions as *de facto* guardians (surrogate decision makers). However, guardians, including those who are court-appointed, may not always act in the person's best interest and may have conflicting philosophies, values, and motives.

Psychiatric Hospitalization of Older Adults

Many states have a statute that outlines the procedures for voluntary and involuntary admission to psychiatric hospitals. To be admitted voluntarily, the individual must demonstrate the capacity to provide informed consent. In the event an individual needs psychiatric treatment and refuses or is incapable of providing informed consent, the person may be involuntarily committed for evaluation and treatment.

Criteria for involuntary commitment usually include danger to oneself, danger to others, or an inability to adequately care for oneself because of mental illness. Continued hospitalization in a secured psychiatric facility may be one of the few psychiatric options available to service recipients, as reimbursement frequently shapes service options. There are few other treatment options within the community that are reimbursed through Medicare or private insurance companies that provide effective intervention. Many geriatric admissions to psychiatric hospitals are frequently discharged to other healthcare facilities such as nursing homes, particularly if these individuals are unmarried and do not have a family.

Determining Mental Competence and Capacity

Determining mental capacity is not always easy. Cognitive function is not always consistent, and there are degrees of mental capacity in older adults. When estimating a person's mental capacity, social workers should consider any temporary or remediable factors that can affect a person's decision-making abilities in a specific situation. For example, a person in familiar surroundings may have the mental capacity to make decisions and be able to function adequately, but that same individual may become confused when newly admitted to a hospital or nursing home. The side effects of medications may also cause cognitive changes. The story of Joan shows the importance of considering all factors that may affect mental competence and capacity in a given situation.

In my work as a hospital social worker, it was not unusual to receive a referral from a physician asking me to initiate guardianship proceedings for a hospitalized patient. On this day, the patient was an 80-year-old woman, Joan, who was recovering from abdominal surgery. The physician's referral requested that a guardianship be obtained so that it would be possible for him to discharge Joan involuntarily to a nursing home.

Joan greeted me when I entered her room and asked if she could go home. I administered a Mini-Mental State Examination (MMSE) to screen for cognitive impairment. Joan exhibited some confusion and appeared slightly disoriented but was verbally and socially appropriate. I looked at her medical chart to review her pre-op history and the physician notes and found no documentation stating that she had a history of cognitive impairment prior to her surgery.

Because it had only been 2 days since Joan's surgery, I began to suspect that she might be experiencing a postoperative psychosis. This was not the first time that I had seen this condition in a geriatric patient following surgery. A postoperative psychosis often occurs as a result of the effects of anesthesia and may last anywhere from a day to several months. The fact that Joan had no prior symptoms of cognitive impairment suggested that her confusion and disorientation were related to her surgery and would probably lessen over the next few days.

When I shared this possibility with Joan's physician, he disagreed, saying that he wanted to discharge her as soon as possible to a nursing home. To do this, he would have to request an emergency guardianship. As ordered, I began the guardianship process. By the time the court examination was completed, Joan's condition had cleared, and she was found to be legally competent. Joan returned to her home.

Several criteria must be met for a person to be considered mentally competent. Mentally competent persons should be able to

1. Understand and express the choice they are being asked to make

2. Demonstrate an understanding of their condition, including diagnosis, prognosis, and possible treatments

3. Balance the benefits and risks of available choices

4. Communicate the rationale for their choice

Whenever a person's competence is called into question, the following principles of decisional capacity can be used to guide the social worker:

- Decisional capacity is specific to the situation.

- When determining whether a person has the adequate capacity to make a decision, the possible risks, benefits, and strain of the proposed intervention or treatment should be considered, along with the consequences of the client's choice.

- When decisional capacity is in question, neurological and psychiatric evaluations are recommended.

- Poor judgment is not synonymous with impaired capacity.

- Mentally competent individuals who are aware of the consequences of their choices can assume the risks.

- When the person has mental capacity but makes a decision that is against medical advice, there still may be areas of agreement with care professionals that will support a collaborative (although possibly less optimal) plan of care. For example, a person diagnosed with prediabetes may choose to use diet and exercise rather than medication to reduce his or her A1C level.

- When capacity is indeterminate, other factors external to the client are given consideration (e.g., caregivers, family).

Client advocacy in social work involves not only supporting older adults to express their wishes and desires, but also ensuring that their informed consent is legitimate and that they are given the choice about treatments and interventions whenever possible. If competence in some abilities is questionable, the individual's remaining abilities should still be respected.

CHAPTER NOTES

1. Carstensen, L.L., Edelstein, B.A., & Dornbrand, L. (1995). *The practical handbook of clinical gerontology.* Thousand Oaks, CA: SAGE Publications, Inc.
2. Kennedy, G.J. (2000). *Geriatric mental health care.* New York: The Guilford Press.
3. Alzheimer's Association. (2018). 2018 Alzheimer's disease facts and figures. *Alzheimer's & Dementia: The Journal of the Alzheimer's Association, 14*(3), 367–429. doi:https://doi.org/10.1016/j.jalz.2018.02.001
4. Scanland, S., & Bielinski, T. (2017). Differentiating dementias: Focus on accurate dementia diagnosis, Part Two. *Today's Geriatric Medicine, 10*(3), 18–22.
5. Goodman, R.A., Lochner, K.A., Thambisetty, M., Wingo, T.S., Posner, S.F., & Ling, S.M. (2017). Prevalence of dementia subtypes in United States Medicare fee-for-service beneficiaries, 2011-2013. *Alzheimer's & Dementia: The Journal of the Alzheimer's Association, 13*(1), 28–37. doi:10.1016/j.jalz.2016.04.002.
6. Florida Guardianship Law, Fla. Stat. § 744.304, § 744.312, § 744.331, § 744.341, § 744.361 (1995).

CHAPTER 8

Social Support

KEY POINTS

- Family members provide most of the care to older adults.

- Responsibility for the care of elders varies among families from diverse cultural, racial, and ethnic backgrounds, and care may also be provided by extended family.

- Family life has created additional roles during older adulthood. The additional responsibilities of caregiving for grandchildren or adult children with intellectual or physical disabilities intersect with the experience of growing older.

SOCIAL SUPPORT IS MEANINGFUL, appropriate, and protective feedback from the social environment that enables a person to cope with intermittent or continual environmental stressors.[1] Although many environmental stressors cannot be prevented, a person's social support can be modified and, in most cases, improved. Several elements of an older adult's social support network should be assessed.

- *Roles and available attachments*: the individuals and groups of individuals within the social network available to the older adult, such as spouse, children, and siblings.

- *Frequency of social interaction*: the actual number of contacts and interactions within the social network; for example, how often an older adult speaks in person or by telephone with members of the social network.

- *Perceived social support:* the older adult's subjective evaluation and perception of a reliable social network, ease of interaction with the network, a sense of belonging to the network, and a feeling of comfort with network members.

- *Instrumental support:* concrete and observable services provided to the older adult by the social network, such as meal preparation, transportation, or personal care.

Family Support and Caregiving

Family members provide most of the care to older adults. Approximately 52 million caregivers in the United States provide care to adults with a disability or illness.[2] Family support is sometimes referred to as an informal support system. An older adult's informal support may be a spouse, partner, family member, friend, or neighbor. These are unpaid persons who aid with activities of daily living and/or medical tasks.

Although most family caregivers continue to be women (75%), there has been an increase in the number of men who are in this role. Over half of caregivers are employed, balancing their responsibilities as an employee and as a caregiver. Research has demonstrated that work productivity is diminished when an individual takes on the role of caregiver. As caregiving responsibilities become greater, there is a likelihood that the caregiver will have to reduce work hours, or in some cases, leave the workforce. The reduction or loss of income can have serious economic consequences for the caregiver's later years, affecting social security and pension benefits.[3]

Families are the primary caregivers for adults with intellectual and developmental disabilities (I/DD). About 76% of individuals with I/DD reside at home. In 25% of these homes, the family caregiver is over 60 years of age.[3] The increase in lifespan for persons with I/DD now means that, for many parents, providing in-home care for a daughter or son is a lifelong responsibility. Providing care becomes more difficult for many older parents as they experience a decline in their health, strength, and patience. When parents become ill or die, a sibling usually becomes the caregiver. For the sibling who assumes the responsibility of providing day-to-day care, there can be conflict between family and career responsibilities.

The increased longevity of the population and the growing number of families having children later in life have led to an increase in another group of caregivers: those who are caring for their parents while simultaneously providing care to their children or grandchildren. This phenomenon is referred to as the "sandwich generation." Nearly half (47%) of middle-aged adults have a parent aged 65 or older and are either raising a young child or financially supporting a grown child.[4]

Family support, including support from extended families, often helps in meeting the needs of older adults from diverse cultural, racial, and ethnic backgrounds. In some cultures, it is the family's responsibility to care for older family members, and it is widely believed that many ethnic subgroups provide better intergenerational support than white Americans. This portrayal may be overly simplistic, and the differences between groups may not be as large as stated. It is important to stress that regardless of race or ethnicity, most of the care that older adults receive is provided by family members.

In comparison with other minority populations, African American elders interact more with family members and report higher levels of support from them.[5,6] Older African Americans are more likely to live with their children and relatives. This may be because of the exchange of financial and child care support between elders and younger family members. Extended family members and members of the community also assume caregiving roles similar to family members. The increased mobility of young African Americans to urban areas has resulted in a decrease in a familial source of support, causing elders to rely on other means of support, such as friends and religious and community organizations. Intergenerational conflict has become more common recently, particularly among African American families who have been affected by the drug epidemic. Many older African Americans have lost children to drugs or crime and have assumed primary caretaking responsibilities for their grandchildren.[7]

Latinos/Latinas have the highest reported prevalence of caregiving of any ethnic group (21%).[8] They are also more likely to be a primary caregiver and are often more reluctant to send their elders to nursing homes or assisted living. This reluctance stems from the belief that not accepting the role of caregiver could bring shame on the family and the understanding of caregiving as a shared responsibility among relatives, especially female siblings. As with other minority groups, stereotypes about Latino/Latina culture persist regarding the family's role in caring for older adults. Although the family plays an important role in caregiving, it has become more difficult for younger relatives to care for elders.

There are also differences in interpersonal relationships and social support across ethnic subgroups. For example, of all ethnic-minority subgroups, Chinese American elders are the most likely to live with their children.[9] Yet, they often report that they have little contact with their children. This paradox may stem from differing expectations among younger and older generations. Many Chinese American elders expect to receive respect and care from younger relatives when they grow old and feel a sense of abandonment when that does not occur. Their younger relatives' assimilation to Western culture may also threaten the self-esteem of Chinese American elders and cause intergenerational conflict.[10]

Similar to other racial and ethnic groups, most Native American elders are cared for by informal caregivers. Caregivers are typically members of extended, multigenerational families who share a value orientation that is focused on the needs of the group rather than the individual. A coping strategy unique to Native Americans has been labeled "passive forbearance," which is defined as accepting and adapting to the caregiving role rather than trying to control it.[11] Recently, family support for Native American elders has been affected by the migration of the younger generations, who are relocating from reservations to urban areas.[12]

When working with older members of the LGBTQ population, social workers must give special consideration to their formal and informal support networks. Nearly two-thirds (64%) of the LGBTQ population say that they have a "chosen family," defined as a group of people to whom they are emotionally close and consider "family" even though not biologically or legally related.[13] Older LGBTQ adults may be more reluctant to disclose their sexual orientation to a social worker than would a younger person and may not provide accurate information about their family situation.

Although it has been the norm in several cultures for the family to care for older relatives, recent changes in societal patterns and family structure mean that social workers need to look beyond stereotypical assumptions. The idea that members of the younger generation are culturally mandated to take care of their parents is deeply ingrained in several cultures. However, that tradition is being eroded by the increasing number of families that are geographically dispersed or in situations in which both spouses must work.

In many cases, an older adult depends on the extended family for assistance. Family members such as nieces, nephews, and cousins, as well as close friends, should be considered essential participants in the care plan. At the same time, the limitations of family and friends as major resources need to be considered, as they, too, might be struggling with their own issues. Each individual family situation should be assessed to ensure the appropriate balance of formal and informal support. An effective care plan collectively considers the client's care needs, stress on the caregivers, and the family's economic situation.

Caregiver Burden and Abuse

Caregiver burden is the stress or strain that caregivers experience from the challenges of caregiving.[14] It is the caregiver's perception of the burden (i.e., subjective burden) that determines the overall impact of caregiving on the caregiver. Families often struggle to provide care to older family members for many years, sometimes resorting to institutional care when they are emotionally and physically exhausted. The role of caregiver does not end with placement of a family member in an assisted living or long-term care setting. Although the caregiving responsibilities may change from providing direct care to care management and monitoring, some degree of burden and stress continues for the caregiver and family. Social workers should consider anyone involved in the care of an older adult, either directly or indirectly, to be a caregiver. Evaluating that person's role in caregiving, the stress or effects of the caregiver situation, and his or her strengths and needs requires sensitivity and knowledge of caregiver issues.

Older adults who are frail or have illnesses or disabilities are increasingly dependent on others as they lose their cognitive and physical abilities. This leaves them particularly vulnerable to abuse and neglect by caregivers, who are often overwhelmed by caregiving responsibilities. Elder abuse includes physical abuse, emotional abuse, sexual abuse, exploitation, neglect, and abandonment (see Table 8.1). According to the National Council on Aging, almost 60% of domestic elder abuse and neglect cases involve a family member. Two-thirds of perpetrators are adult children or spouses.[15] Because elder abuse is most often at the hands of family members, the shame of being abused may impair the victim's ability to divulge the information. Victims of elder abuse are often reluctant to report the abuse for fear of retribution or being taken from the home and institutionalized. Embarrassment, denial, reliance on the abuser, and a wish to protect abusive family members are also reasons for not reporting.

Social isolation and cognitive impairment are two risk factors for elder abuse. Interpersonal violence also occurs at higher rates among adults with disabilities. Table 8.1 describes the types and warning signs of elder abuse.

Table 8.1   Detection of Elder Abuse and Neglect

Types of Abuse	Symptoms of Abuse
Physical abuse (inflicting physical pain or injury)	• Bruises • Pressure marks on skin • Broken bones • Abrasions • Burns • History of frequent hospital emergency room visits
Sexual abuse (touching, fondling, intercourse, or any other sexual contact with an older adult who is unable to understand, unwilling to consent, threatened, or physically forced)	• Genital or breast bruising • Genital or anal bleeding
Emotional abuse (verbal assaults; threats of harm, harassment, or intimidation)	• Frequent arguments between the family member and older adult • Persistent suspicion or fear of a family member • Unexplained withdrawal from normal activities • Changes in mood; frequent, unexplained crying
Financial exploitation (misuse or withholding of resources)	• Sudden changes in financial situations • Unexplained bank withdrawals or selling of assets
Neglect (denying an older adult medication, medical care, shelter, food, a therapeutic device, or other physical assistance; exposing the person to the risk of harm)	• Poor hygiene, unexplained weight loss, unattended medical needs, skin breakdown • Contracture of extremeties (e.g., hands, arms, feet, or legs)

Detection of abuse or neglect begins with history taking. Inconsistencies regarding injury, a history of frequent hospital visits, and claims that the person is "accident prone" should all raise concerns. Medication-related problems (e.g., failure to take medications as prescribed) that lead to doctor or hospital visits should also raise suspicions. Isolation from social support (formal and informal) is another risk factor that should be considered. Caregiver pathology, such as substance abuse, mental illness, or a history of criminal offenses, should be noted. An assessment of caregiver burden is important for determining the level of caregiver stress. Information about the older adult's living situation that includes household composition and description of living quarters will provide details about the adequacy of the environment.

When abuse or neglect is suspected, a home visit is necessary. Depending on the social worker's role and job responsibilities, this visit can either be conducted by the social worker or referred to the appropriate community resource, such as Adult Protective Services or a home health agency. The in-home assessment will detect needs and recommend assistance to the often-overwhelmed caregiver. A dirty, unsafe environment; absence of assistive or medical equipment; and lack of food should be noted. If the caregiver repeatedly cancels the house-call appointment, this should be cause for concern. If there is evidence of abuse or neglect by the caregiver or another family member, social workers and other healthcare professionals are mandated to report it to the appropriate agency. Immediate intervention may be necessary and should not jeopardize the safety of the older adult. If removal of the individual from his or her environment is warranted, supportive help or referrals should be provided to the caregiver and family members.

Support from Friends and Neighbors

The mobile nuclear family system can create a sense of isolation for older adults. Children and grandchildren may live miles away and maintain infrequent contact. The likelihood of living in a family household diminishes with age from 73% among people aged 65–74 to 48% for those 85 and older.[16] Most people have some type of support network but are often unaware of their potential support system or may be reluctant to ask for help. Although friends and neighbors may be unable or unwilling to assist with day-to-day care, they might be able to provide some transportation, socialization, or telephone reassurance. Other sources of social support include religious organizations, apartment staff, and support groups. I witnessed a neighborhood support system firsthand with my own grandfather.

As I walked into the funeral home, I was struck by the sight of a frail older man standing by the side of my grandfather's casket. He stood for a while, looking into the casket, using his cane for balance. As he turned and slowly made his way toward me, I realized that it was Johnny, the last Canasta player.

The group had gathered every Wednesday evening for over 20 years to play cards. The three couples had moved to the neighborhood in different stages of their lives, some with children in their teens and one whose family included grandchildren. The common threads that bound them together and created lasting friendships were the stories they shared as immigrants who came to the United States from England and Ireland when they were children and young adults. They were working-class families—carpenters, gardeners, house painters, and housekeepers, making just enough money to build their small houses and raise their families.

In times of loss as well as during periods of illness and family crises, the group's members provided support to one another. Over the years, the group became smaller, some of the friends moving into nursing homes and eventually passing away, leaving just Johnny and my grandfather. Soon after my grandmother passed away, my grandfather moved to the next town to live with his daughter, but he and Johnny continued to get together to share memories and discuss the state of the world.

Many older LGBTQ adults rely on close friends for support. A high proportion of this population lives alone rather than with a partner or spouse. Older LGBTQ adults report having close friends that are a source of emotional support. They often live with friends, are likely to have discussed their end-of-life preferences with close friends, and are more likely to depend on a friend as a caregiver.[16]

For some older LGBTQ adults who married and raised children with heterosexual partners, an LGBTQ identity may not be lifelong. At midlife or later, acceptance of an LGBTQ identity may have become possible. Older LGBTQ adults also have additional identities and minority statuses, such as ethnicity, socioeconomic status, and religious background. These intersections are important to understanding the older LGBTQ adult.

When assessing social support, social workers should avoid assumptions based on race, ethnicity, sexual orientation, or any other single identity. Rather, they should consider caregiving and support options across the diverse social networks that make up each older adult's world.

CHAPTER NOTES

1. Blazer, D. (1998). *Emotional problems in later life: Intervention strategies for professional caregivers.* New York: Springer Publishing Company.

2. Coughlin, J. (2010). Estimating the impact of caregiving and employment on well-being. *Outcomes & Insights in Health Management, 2*(1), 1–7.

3. Family Caregiver Alliance (2016). National Center on Caregiving. Retrieved from https://www.caregiver.org.

4. Heller, T. (2014). People with intellectual and developmental disabilities growing old: An overview. *Impact, 23*(1), 2–3.

5. Parker, K.E., & Patten, E. (2013). *The sandwich generation: Rising financial burdens for middle-aged Americans.* Washington, DC: Pew Research Center, Social & Demographic Trends. Retrieved from https://www.pewsocialtrends.org/2013/01/30/the-sandwich-generation/

6. Carstensen, L.L., Edelstein, B.A., & Dornbrand, L. (1995). *The practical handbook of clinical gerontology.* Thousand Oaks, CA: SAGE Publications, Inc.

7. Lipscomb, R.C. (2005). The challenges of African American grandparents raising their grandchildren. *Race, Gender and Class, 12*(2), 163–177.

8. Markides, K.S., & Mindel, C. (1987). *Aging and ethnicity (SAGE Library Social Research Edition).* Newbury Park, CA: SAGE Publications, Inc.

9. Evercare & National Alliance for Caregiving. (2008). *Evercare® study of Hispanic family caregiving in the U.S.: Findings from a national study.* Retrieved from https://www.caregiving.org/data/Hispanic_Caregiver_Study_web_ENG_FINAL_11_04_08.pdf

10. Raskind, M., & Peskind, E.R. (1992). Alzheimer's disease and other dementing disorders. In J.E. Birren, R.B. Sloane, B.D. Lebowitz, D.E. Deutchman, M. Wykle, & N.R. Hooyman (Eds.), *Handbook of mental health and aging* (2nd ed.) (pp. 478–516). San Diego, CA: Academic Press.

11. For further reading on Asian caregivers, see Ishii-Kuntz, M. (1997). Intergenerational relationships among Chinese, Japanese, and Korean Americans. *Family Relations, 46*(1), 23–32.

12. Goins, R.T., Spencer, S.M., McGuire, L.C., Goldberg, J., Wen, Y., & Henderson, J.A. (2011). Adult caregiving among American Indians: The role of cultural factors. *The Gerontologist, 51*(3), 310–320.

13. For further reading on Native American caregivers, see Hennessy, C.H., & John, R. (1996). American Indian family caregivers' perceptions of burden and needed support services. *Journal of Applied Gerontology, 15*(3), 275–293.

14. The MetLife Mature Market Institute® & The American Society on Aging (ASA). (2010). *Still out, still aging: The MetLife study of lesbian, gay, bisexual, and transgender baby boomers.* Westport, CT: MetLife. Retrieved from https://www.asaging.org/sites/default/files/files/mmi-still-out-still-aging.pdf

15. For further reading on caregiver burden, see Slaboda, J., Fail, R., Norman, G., & Meier, D.E. (January 11, 2018). A study of family caregiver burden and the imperative of practice change to address family caregivers' unmet needs [Blog post]. Retrieved from https://www.healthaffairs.org/do/10.1377/hblog20180105.914873/full/; Kaplan, M. (1996). *Clinical practice with caregivers of dementia patients.* Bristol, PA: Taylor & Francis; Zarit, S.H., Reever, K.E., & Bach-Peterson, J. (1980). Relatives of the impaired elderly: Correlates of feelings of burden. *The Gerontologist, 20*(6), 649–655.

16. National Council on Aging (NCOA). (n.d.). Elder abuse facts. Retrieved from https://www.ncoa.org/public-policy-action/elder-justice/elder-abuse-facts/

CHAPTER 9

Economic Resources

KEY POINTS

- Financial circumstances often impact the health status and behavior of an older adult.

- Higher poverty rates are found among older women, minorities, and persons with chronic illnesses.

- The life change of retirement is accompanied by psychological and financial adjustments.

THE ECONOMIC STATUS of older adults is varied, with the largest percentage of people with incomes below the poverty level represented by women, minorities, and the oldest old. Women who entered the labor force at the beginning of childbearing have faced career interruptions and tend to have diminished income later in life. Unpredictable or non-normative life events, such as getting divorced or losing a job, also have a significant effect on the life course and economic resources. Research has shown that these life events can cause a significant downturn in personal health and can profoundly affect an individual's financial status during retirement.[1]

For the 65-and-older population, 22% of men and 14% of women are in the labor force. Although less than the total population, these percentages are consistent with trends showing an increasing number of people aged 65 and older in the workplace. Although the labor force consisted of a higher proportion of men for all age groups, this difference was more pronounced for the oldest-old age groups. For those aged 75–84, the percentage of men in the workforce (11%) was almost twice the percentage of women (6%), and for those aged 85 and older, the percentage of men was double (4%) that of women (2%).[2]

The passage of the Social Security Act of 1935 (PL 74–271) and the growth of private pensions have improved the economic status of older adults in the United States. Social Security is the most common type of household income for older adults, received by 90% of persons aged 65 and older.[3] Poverty rates declined sharply during the 1970s following the indexing of Social Security benefits to the cost of living. This has helped to reduce the percentage of older adults living below the poverty level (less than $10,458 annual income in 2010 for a person aged 65 and older) from 15% to 9%.[4] Older women who have never married have the highest poverty rate at 29%, compared to 21% for never-married older males.[5]

Economic Resources of Minority Elders

Higher poverty rates are found among older women, minorities, and individuals with chronic illnesses. Members of these groups often have not held jobs that allowed them to collect maximum Social Security benefits or private pensions or to accumulate much wealth.

African American elders have the highest poverty rate, at 18.7%.[6] Older African Americans typically experienced disadvantage in the workplace, with prejudice or discrimination constricting their opportunities for advancement. In previous decades, African American women were too often confined to the secondary job market and hired for domestic positions (e.g., housekeeper, maid) that paid low wages with little or no benefits and poor job security.

The poverty rate in 2016 for Hispanic Americans aged 65 and older was 17.4%.[6] Hispanic older adults are the least prepared for retirement of any ethnic minority group, with most living in economic insecurity. This is partly because most Hispanic older adults depend solely on Social Security benefits, often receiving lower payments than other beneficiaries. These low-income levels place Hispanic older adults on a thin line of solvency, where any economic change, such as an illness or an increase in housing costs, could plunge them into poverty or even hunger.

Asian elders had one of the lowest poverty rates at 11.8%.[6] Statistics on Asian Americans show a population with high education levels, earning potential, and net worth, but this data obscures a growing population of Asian American, Native Hawaiian, and Pacific Islander elders that lack the financial resources of younger generations. Between 2009 and 2014, the poverty rate increased 40% for Asian American elders and 50% for

Native Hawaiian and Pacific Islander elders.[7] Access to affordable housing is often a factor in their financial security. Asian American elders are likely to move to Asian American cultural centers, such as Los Angeles, San Francisco, and New York, for social engagement and social support. These are cities with expensive housing prices, which makes it difficult for older adults on a fixed income to maintain economic stability.

As a group, LGBTQ older adults experience economic disparities. They may be disproportionately affected by poverty and mental health issues because of a lifetime of stressors associated with their minority status. Members of this population often face dual discrimination because of their age and sexual orientation or gender identity.

Financing Healthcare

Medicare was passed as a special section of the Social Security Act (Title XVIII) and began in 1966. It was developed in response to the growing healthcare needs of older persons and the limited incomes of older adults. In 1972, the program expanded to include older persons who are not eligible for Social Security but who are willing to pay a monthly premium for health services.[8] Medicare has proved to be an important means of guaranteeing access to medical care for older adults, but it was never designed to address the costs of long-term care. Most older adults expect to rely on Medicare to pay for their personal long-term care needs. They believe that their health insurance benefits will pay for such costs, even though neither of these benefits typically covers long-term care expenses. Only 1 in 7 older adults have purchased long-term care insurance. Approximately 30% say they expect to rely on Medicaid.[9]

Medicaid is the primary payer for 51% of recipients of long-term care services.[10] A government program supported by federal and state funds, Medicaid was created in 1965 to provide healthcare for the poor. Over the years, it has become the primary government mechanism to pay for long-term care for older adults and persons with disabilities. Medicaid is a means-tested entitlement program, using eligibility rules based on income and assets.

Many older adults who do not qualify for Medicaid still do not have enough funds to pay for long-term care themselves. They must either struggle to pay for home-based care or do what is necessary to obtain Medicaid. This means "spending down" a lifetime of accumulated assets to become impoverished and thereby eligible for Medicaid benefits.

Medicaid has become the public program of last resort to pay long-term care costs. It is the fastest-growing component of state budgets, and it is increasingly becoming an old-age program.

Financial Stress in Late Life

A decrease in financial independence is a major cause of stress in older adults. The most common causes of financial stress are financial changes following retirement, increased medical costs, and increased care costs for ill family members. Researchers have observed that older adults with greater financial liabilities are more likely to experience symptoms of depression, anxiety, self-destructiveness, anger, and suicidal behaviors.[11-13]

The amount of stress people experience as a result of their financial circumstances is subjective; each person will react and feel differently about debt or their personal cost of living. Financial stress, defined as the psychological stress that arises from one's financial conditions, includes subjective feelings or thoughts about finances that may lead to fear, anxiety, frustration, and anger. Financial stress can restrict an individual's ability to solve problems, meet financial demands, and afford the necessities of life.

Financial stress can also impact an older adult's physical health. Chronic heart disease, high blood pressure, cancer, arthritis, digestive tract problems, and other symptoms indicative of chronic stress are common among those with a high level of financial stress. Stress can also impact health indirectly by influencing health behaviors, including diet, physical activity, and substance abuse. Poor health, in turn, can negatively influence economic status by limiting earnings and depleting savings, thereby encouraging a cycle of decline.[11,14]

The strong correlation between financial stress levels and self-rated physical and mental health suggests the importance of managing financial stress for older adults. Social work intervention should address debt reduction and financial management while using health-promotion strategies to reduce the stress that arises from financial obligations.

Retirement

In our society, retirement is seen as a rite of passage, marking the end of a productive economic life and the beginning of a life outside the system of economic production. Work is often viewed as a measure of a person's worth, and the worker's identity is linked to his or her occupation.

The more a person's life revolves around work, the more difficult retirement can be. Occupations also include involvement in organizations such as unions, professional associations, and clubs, making retirement more than just the loss of a job.

If the later years do not offer exciting new roles to replace the occupational roles lost in retirement, the retiree often continues to identify with his or her earlier occupation in order to maintain a positive self-image. This is especially true for those who had strong professional identities, such as physicians or attorneys. Depression related to retirement may have more to do with physical health and income loss than with social factors. Poor physical health often leads to retirement, so increased depression after retirement may be a result of medical illness rather than the retirement itself.

Retirement is usually accompanied by little fanfare and public notice compared with other major turning points in life, such as marriage and graduation. The process of retirement (Figure 9.1) begins when a person recognizes that someday he or she will retire.

Retirement planning involves developing a plan for "life after work." What most people think about when planning for retirement is "How much money will I need?" Too few consider the psychological adjustments that accompany this life change. These include coping with the loss of a career identity, replacing workplace support networks, spending more time with a spouse or family, and finding new ways to stay active.

Post-retirement relationships and obligations to family members may cause family resentment and conflict. Many retirees feel pressured by family members to plan their retirement based on family needs, such as babysitting grandchildren or becoming caregivers for other family members. Conflict often develops between spouses, particularly if the retiree spent most of his or her career away from home and is used to exercising authority in the workplace. I once had a client who grew frustrated with her newly retired husband. "For 35 years, I kept the house clean and did the cooking, and now he is telling me how to vacuum the carpet and make dinner," she stated.

Figure 9.1   The Retirement Process

People with certain personality characteristics—such as being competitive and assertive—have more difficulty adjusting to retirement. Many take on new jobs after retiring from their primary careers through part-time work, a temporary job, or self-employment. The Sloan Center on Aging & Work and the Families and Work Institute report that one in five workers has a post-retirement job and that 75% of workers expect to work or transition to a second career at some point after they retire.[15] In the end, it is important for people to invest time in developing an awareness of their social and psychological post-retirement needs in addition to developing a financial plan.

CHAPTER NOTES

1. Herpolsheimer, L.J. (2015). *Financial stress: How older adults' health is affected.* (Doctoral dissertation). Retrieved from https://soar.wichita.edu/handle/10057/11596

2. Kromer, B., & Howard, D. (2013). *Labor force participation and work status of people 65 years and older* (American Community Survey Briefs, ACSBR/11-09). Washington, DC: U.S. Census Bureau.

3. Roberts, A.W., Ogunwole, S.U., Blakeslee, L., & Rabe, M.A. (2018). *The population 65 years and older in the United States: 2016* (American Community Survey Reports, ACS-38). Washington, DC: U.S. Census Bureau.

4. Federal Interagency Forum on Aging-Related Statistics. (2012). *Older Americans 2012: Key indicators of well-being.* Washington, DC: U.S. Government Publishing Office. Retrieved from https://agingstats.gov/docs/PastReports/2012/OA2012.pdf

5. Morrissey, M. (2016). Women over 65 are more likely to be poor than men, regardless of race, educational background, and marital status. Economic Policy Institute. Retrieved from https://www.epi.org/publication/women-over-65-are-more-likely -to-in-poverty-than-men.

6. U.S. Census Bureau & U.S. Bureau of Labor Statistics (2017). *Current Population Survey, Annual Social and Economic (ASEC) Supplement POV01: Age and sex of all people, family members and unrelated individuals iterated by income-to-poverty ratio and race.* Washington, DC: U.S. Census Bureau. Retrieved from https://www.census.gov /data/tables/time-series/demo/income-poverty/cps-pov/pov-01.html

7. National Coalition for Asian Pacific American Community Development (CAPCD). (2016). *Findings on financial security for AAPI seniors & their families: A landscape assessment & community survey results.* Retrieved from https://www.aarp.org/content /dam/aarp/home-and-family/asian-community/2016/09/capacd-report-aarp-2016. pdf?intcmp=AE-ASIAN-COMMUNITY.

8. Gottlieb, G.L. (1996). Financial issues. In J. Sadavoy, L.W. Lazarus, L. Jarvik, & G.T. Grossberg (Eds.), *Comprehensive review of geriatric psychiatry. II* (2nd ed.). (pp. 1065–1085). Washington, DC: American Psychiatric Press.

9. The MetLife Mature Market Institute® & The American Society on Aging (ASA). (2010). *Still out, still aging: The MetLife study of lesbian, gay, bisexual, and transgender baby boomers.* Westport, CT: MetLife. Retrieved from https://www.asaging.org /sites/default/files/files/mmi-still-out-still-aging.pdf

10. Reaves, E.L., & Musumeci, M. (2015). The Kaiser Commission on Medicaid and the uninsured. https://www.kff.org/infographic/medicaids-role-in-nursing-home-care.

11. Drentea, P. (2000). Age, debt, and anxiety. *Journal of Health and Social Behavior*, *41*(4), 437–450.

12. Ferraro, K.F., & Su, Y. (1999). Financial strain, social relations, and psychological distress among older people: A cross-cultural analysis. *Journal of Gerontology: Social Sciences, 54B*(1), S3–S15.

13. Morris, D.C. (1997). Health, finances, religious involvement, and life satisfaction of older adults. *Journal of Religious Gerontology, 2*(3), 3–17.

14. Kahn, J.R., & Fazio, E.M. (2005). Economic status over the life course and racial disparities in health. *Journals of Gerontology Series B: Psychological Sciences and Social Sciences, 60*, 76–84.

15. Brown, M., Aumann, K., Pitt-Catsouphes, M., Galinsky, E., & Bond, J.T. (2010). *Working in retirement: A 21ˢᵗ century phenomenon.* New York: Families and Work Institute. Retrieved from http://familiesandwork.org/site/research/reports/workingin retirement.pdf

CHAPTER 10

Living Environments

KEY POINTS

- Older adults who remain in their homes report greater life satisfaction and less depression, and they maintain their physical functioning at higher rates than elders who live in long-term care settings.

- Environmental interventions and assistive technologies have been successful in maintaining and/or increasing function for older adults with disabilities.

- Changes in living environment are often challenging for older adults and may result in relocation or transfer trauma.

MOST OLDER ADULTS LIVE INDEPENDENTLY. In fact, only about 5% of individuals over the age of 65 reside in long-term care settings. This figure represents those who reside in a nursing home at any given time. Although the number is small, the risk of spending some time in a nursing home is still great. It is estimated that 43% of people who live to be 65 or older and reside in long-term care settings will spend some time in a nursing home.[1]

The risk of placement in a long-term care setting is related to advancing age, the need for ambulatory assistance, disorientation, living alone, and requiring assistance with activities of daily living. The chance for placement increases if an older adult is unmarried, has no children, and is female.[2] Many admissions to nursing homes are for short-term rehabilitation. These individuals usually return home to their spouse or family.

Long-term care options for an older adult are not only dependent upon the characteristics and needs of the individual, but also upon policy at the federal and state levels. There is no consistent or comprehensive federal policy for long-term care.[3] The evidence for this claim comes from federal programs for older adults, such as Medicare and federal block grants for programs such as Medicaid. Medicaid is the primary payer for 51% of recipients of long-term care services.[4]

Aging in place is a priority for many older adults. The Centers for Disease Control and Prevention defines "aging in place" as the ability to live in one's own home and community safely, independently, and comfortably, regardless of age, income, or ability level.[5] Older adults who remain in their own homes report greater life satisfaction and less depression and maintain their physical functioning at higher rates than elders who reside in assisted living or long-term care settings.[6-8]

Aging in place is not a one-size-fits-all concept. Instead, it reflects the diversity of older adults.[9] Preferences, needs, and access to services differ among older adults depending on their residence in rural or urban settings, income levels, sexual orientation, gender identity, and special circumstances, such as being caregivers of adult children with disabilities or grandparents raising grandchildren. To age in place successfully, the older person must be safe, able to take care of his or her needs, or able to find the resources to fulfill those needs.

Most older adults say that they wish to remain in their own homes until their death, but the likelihood that they may experience physical disability, medical conditions, and cognitive issues in their later years makes that scenario less probable. The probability of becoming disabled in at least two activities of daily living or becoming cognitively impaired is 68% for people aged 65 and older.[10] In addition to personal life events, environmental changes such as loss of support from neighbors who move away or die, an increase in neighborhood crime rates, or redevelopment that results in a loss of neighborhood stores or services may also affect the ability of an older adult to remain in his or her home.

The concepts of "livable communities" and "healthy homes" have been promoted for older adults and persons with disabilities. As people age and require more support with activities of daily living, they may require modifications to their homes and communities that allow them to remain in their preferred settings. Environmental interventions to adapt or modify living environments and assistive technologies have led to positive effects on functioning and reduced mortality for persons with Alzheimer's disease, along with decreased stress for their caregivers. Gitlin and Corcoran[11,12] conducted a series of studies to test a home environmental intervention program for older adults with Alzheimer's disease and their caregivers. The intervention focused on enabling the caregiver and client to solve functional and behavioral problems by simplifying tasks, adjusting environmental stimuli, removing dangerous objects, and using assistive technologies and environmental interventions. Findings suggest that this environmental approach had a positive impact on both the caregiver and the person with dementia, slowing the rate of functional decline and enhancing caregiver self-efficacy.

Environmental interventions and assistive technologies have also been found to maintain and/or increase function for older adults with intellectual and developmental disabilities (I/DD). Legislation and social activism movements have promoted the deinstitutionalization of people with I/DD. This movement has also established the right of the I/DD population to live in the community and to receive supportive resources, including assistive technologies and environmental modifications. As defined by the Developmental Disabilities Assistance and Bill of Rights Act of 2000 (PL 106-402), assistive technology is "any item, piece of equipment, or product system, whether acquired commercially, modified, or customized, that is used to increase, maintain, or improve functional capabilities of individuals with developmental disabilities."[13] Although not specified in the legislation, environmental modifications, such as grab bars, ramps, lifts, and modifications to building interiors and exteriors, are often used in conjunction with assistive technology.

Living Arrangements for Older Adults

Although the most common representation of aging in place is an individual living in his or her own single-family house, other examples include independent living or assisted-living options within residential senior living communities. There are several types of residential care options available in most states. The names used to refer to each type of residence vary from state to state. In addition, some types of living arrangements are licensed and required to follow set regulations.

Senior Apartments

These settings provide individual apartments that contain cooking facilities. There may be common areas available for residents to socialize, but staff-directed activities are not always offered. This type of housing is not licensed and may not have staff onsite 24 hours a day. Generally, there is no financial assistance available to pay the rent, but some senior apartments are designated for low-income older adults under the federal Housing and Urban Development (HUD) program.

Assisted Living

These settings provide a room (private or shared), meals, and the presence of 24-hour staff, with the amount of care provided varying from setting to setting. Nursing care is not provided in assisted living. A structured activity program is available. In most states, assisted living facilities must be licensed by the state depending on the number of residents. Payment is generally limited to private pay, although Medicaid waivers are available in some states to qualifying individuals.

Continuing Care Retirement Communities (CCRCs)

Also referred to as Life Plan Communities, CCRCs are a prime example of a setting that allows an individual to age in place. CCRCs provide all of the levels of care within one residential community. However, the resident moves to different buildings on the campus to receive different services. In most CCRCs, the older adult must purchase his or her apartment and is then entitled to receive other levels of care as needed. In CCRCs, residents who eventually require some assistance with activities of daily living or rehabilitation therapy are usually able to receive assistance in their apartments.

Adjustment Disorder in Older Adults

When an older adult fails to adjust to a change in his or her living situation, this can be viewed as an adjustment disorder or what is also referred to as relocation or transfer trauma. Adjustment requires coping strategies, which are generally learned responses to stress. Coping strategies are based on life experience, environmental factors, cultural norms, and familial patterns.

For older persons, a disruption in lifelong habits and behavior patterns can lead to adjustment problems. Changes in living situation can be especially difficult. For example, a person who smokes may have problems moving into a residence where smoking indoors is not permitted. Persons with histories of alcohol or drug dependency or emotional problems may find it difficult to live in settings that have strict rules about resident behaviors.

Relocating Elders

Many early studies have substantiated that relocation to a different setting can present severe adjustment problems for older adults, showing increased mortality and morbidity rates among relocated older persons.[14] Although research on some aspects of the effects of relocation was inconclusive (e.g., how to identify those at high risk for trauma), there was general agreement that relocation stress could be reduced by counseling prior to and following the move. I am well acquainted with the adjustment challenges older adults can experience when there are changes in living environment, as I share in my story of working as a relocation counselor in Buffalo.

In the mid-1970s, New York was faced with revelations of widespread fraud and corruption within the state's long-term care industry. The passage of Medicare and Medicaid laws during the 1960s had led to the construction of large nursing homes, most privately owned, that were based on a medical model. An investigation by New York's special deputy attorney, who ran an 18-month undercover operation, resulted in the conviction of more than 50 nursing home officials and suppliers for involvement in extensive kickback schemes. Following the exposure of widespread abuses in the state's nursing homes, the Office of the New York State Special Prosecutor for Nursing Homes, Health, and Social Services was created in 1975.

The scandal in New York drew national attention as the public found out that millions of dollars of Medicaid funds designated for the care of older adults and indigent patients were going to greedy and politically influential nursing home owners and operators. In response to the scandal, New York became the first state in the nation to establish an office to investigate healthcare fraud and abuse. New York's efforts to clean up the state's long-term care industry and restore fiscal integrity to the state's healthcare delivery system would become a model for other states.[15]

It wasn't long before the effects of the nursing home scandal reached the Buffalo area, resulting in the closing of several large nursing facilities. Horrific accounts of residents restrained in wheelchairs without adequate clothing or food while nursing home administrators or owners spent Medicare and Medicaid funds on cruises and expensive cars were described in legal reports and in the media. Consequently, Erie County, where Buffalo is located, lost 250 of its long-term care beds in 1974–1975. The residents of these facilities would all need to be relocated. Additionally, approximately 104 Medicaid recipients, all identified as living in inappropriate settings, were being transitioned from skilled nursing facilities to lower levels of care. These events prompted the Erie County Office for the Aging to start a relocation counseling program in 1974. This project was designed to demonstrate the feasibility of providing centralized relocation services to older adults.[16]

I was hired as one of the four relocation counselors for the project in Buffalo, marking the beginning of my social work career. In the next 15 months, 174 persons were relocated in skilled nursing, health-related, and residential care facilities as well as in noninstitutional settings. Referrals came from agencies and facilities serving older adults as well as older adults themselves and their families. Criteria for admission to the program included being aged 65 or older, a resident of Erie County, and a person identified as being at high risk for trauma from relocation even when other factors indicated that a move to a more appropriate level of care may be desirable. High-risk indicators for trauma included the absence of family or social supports, a history of depression or psychiatric problems, and a negative attitude toward relocation.

After the initial interview by the intake social worker, the screening team, which consisted of a physician, two public health nurses, and the assigned caseworker, evaluated the client's level of care based on specific information related to medication, activities of daily living, adjustment to present setting, and psychological status. Recommendations regarding level of care were then formulated.

In my role as a relocation trauma counselor, I provided support and guidance to clients throughout the relocation process. Recognizing the need to allow clients as much control over the move as possible, I fully informed them of the details of the relocation plan to involve them in the process. Brochures and information were provided concerning the various alternative living arrangements, and the realities of the client's situation were discussed. Clients were taken to at least three residences to provide options from which to choose. It was essential for me to be available prior to, during, and after the actual relocation. This contact helped to reassure the client that there would be continuity in services provided by the project.

My being available to help clients on the first day of relocation helped them establish relationships and become familiar with their new settings and seemed to offset depression and emotional stress. Intensive direct services included post-admission follow-up with clients. Counseling was directed toward helping clients recognize and cope with relocation-associated trauma.

In addition to my role in counseling older adults, I utilized the skills of multidisciplinary healthcare professionals to coordinate client services. For those clients who returned to independent living in the community, it was often necessary to contact agencies and organizations, such as home health agencies, Meals on Wheels, legal services, and community mental health services. For clients who could no longer function in a community setting because of deteriorating physical or mental health, I provided continued support and counseling before and after relocation to the appropriate level of care. Communication with the staff of the new residence was essential, and a residential and social care plan was developed that contained information about the client's needs, desires, ability to cope with problems, and the recommended approach to be utilized by staff at the client's new home. Below is an example of one client's transition.

> Sarah, a 78-year-old widow who resided in a senior citizen's apartment building, was referred to the relocation project by the apartment manager. Formerly an artist and an active community leader, Sarah had become increasingly weak and confused, remaining in her apartment for days at a time. When she did go out, she often wandered up and down the hallways of the building, unable to locate her apartment. Complaints from other tenants and a concern for Sarah's health and safety prompted the manager to request assistance. Sarah's family consisted of one son who had recently undergone surgery for a brain tumor and who was unable to care for his mother. Sarah did not want to leave her home, so I arranged for a homemaker aide to come each day. When it became apparent that 24-hour supervision was necessary, Sarah was relocated to an assisted living facility, where I continued to visit her weekly until the project ended.

In addition to providing direct counseling services, the relocation project conducted two conferences to educate healthcare professionals about safely relocating older adults. The project staff also provided in-service programs to nursing home and hospital staff in Erie County. At the end of the project, 139 women and 35 men had been relocated within skilled nursing, assisted living, and independent living settings. Relocation was not completed for seven clients. Of these, four had deteriorating physical or mental conditions, two would not agree to the move, and one individual died before being transferred. The clients ranged in age from 65 to 103, with the average age being 82.

Advanced age has most often been associated as a risk factor for experiencing relocation trauma. However, our counselors found that age was not a determining factor in the client's adjustment to relocation. Rather, the length of stay and the level of adjustment at the client's residence prior to the move proved to be most important. This was particularly true for clients residing in skilled nursing facilities for several years. Most had been admitted by families no longer able to care for them at home. Over the years, these clients had become increasingly dependent upon staff for help with activities of daily living that they themselves were capable of completing if motivated. These clients required counseling for several months before they could function outside the protective environment of the nursing home. At the time of relocation, most clients had been in their residences from 6 months to 1 year. Five clients living in skilled nursing facilities for 10 years or longer were determined not to need nursing care. Of these, two were not relocated because of severe emotional stress associated with the move. Three-fourths of all the project's clients were relocated to community settings.

Client status was evaluated 2 months after the relocation project ended. Status was determined by how well the client was functioning in his or her new setting. Although the project had officially ended, the relocation counselors continued to visit many of their clients and were able to evaluate their post-relocation adjustment. At the time of evaluation, 103 clients had improved, 60 were stable, and six had deteriorated. Five clients had died following relocation, a relatively low number considering the advanced age and the poor health of many study-group participants.

———————————————

Our experience with the project in Buffalo demonstrated that relocation counseling was an effective tool that could help to alleviate much of the trauma associated with moving. We identified several factors to consider when determining the advisability of relocating an older adult and the need for relocation counseling: the length of stay at the present residence, the personality and psychological status of the individual, the degree of adaptation to the current environment, the existence or absence of family and community support systems, and the amount of control that the individual has in the decision-making process.

CHAPTER NOTES

1. National Institute on Aging. (2017). Residential facilities, assisted living, and nursing homes. Retrieved from https://www.nia.nih.gov/health/residential-facilities -assisted-living-and-nursing-homes.

2. Andel, R., Hyer, K., & Slack, A. (2007). Risk factors for nursing home placement in older adults with and without dementia. *Journal of Aging & Health, 19*(2), 213–228.

3. Somers, F.P. (1991). Long-term care and federal policy. *The American Journal of Occupational Therapy, 45*(7), 628–635.

4. Reaves, E.L., & Musumeci, M. (2015). The Kaiser Commission on Medicaid and the uninsured. https://www.kff.org/infographic/medicaids-role-in-nursing-home-care.

5. Centers for Disease Control and Prevention. (2009). Healthy places terminology. Retrieved from https://www.cdc.gov/healthyplaces/terminology.htm

6. Sharifi, F., Ghaderpanahi, M., & Fakhrzadeh, H. (2012). Older people's mortality index: Development of a practical model for prediction of mortality in nursing homes (Kahrizak Elderly Study). *Geriatrics & Gerontology International, 12*, 36–45.

7. Kang-Yi, C.D., Mandell, D.S., Mui, A.C., & Castle, N.G. (2011). Interaction effect of Medicaid census and nursing home characteristics on quality of psychosocial care for residents. *Health Care Management Review, 36*(1), 47–57.

8. Zuidgeest, M., Delnoij, D.M., Luijkx, K.G., de Boer, D., & Westert, G.P. (2012). Patients' experiences of the quality of long-term care among the elderly: Comparing scores over time. *BMC Health Services Research, 12*(26). doi:10.1186/1472-6963-12-26.

9. Cise, A.C., Ofek, Z., & Lindquist, L.A. (2017). Lifespan planning promotes successful aging in place. *Today's Geriatric Medicine, 10*(3), 25–27.

10. Gillsjö, C., Schwartz-Barcott, D., & von Post, I. (2011). Home: The place the older adult cannot imagine living without. *BMC Geriatrics, 11*(10). doi:10.1186/1471-2318 -11-10.

11. Gitlin, L.N., & Corcoran, M. (1993). Expanding caregiver ability to use environmental solutions for problems of bathing and incontinence in the elderly with dementia. *Technology and Disability, 2*(1), 12–21.

12. Gitlin, L.N., Corcoran, M., Winter, L., Boyce, A, & Hauck, W.W. (2001). A randomized, controlled trial of a home environmental intervention: Effect on efficacy and upset in caregivers and on daily function of persons with dementia. *The Gerontologist, 41*(1), 4–14.

13. Hammel, J., Lai, J.S., & Heller, T. (2002). The impact of assistive technology and environmental interventions on function and living situation status with people who are ageing with developmental disabilities. *Disability and Rehabilitation, 24*(1–3), 93–105.

14. For further reading on relocation trauma, see Reinardy, J.R. (1992). Decisional control in moving to a nursing home: Postadmission adjustment and well-being. *The Gerontologist.* 32(1), 96–103; Hunt, M.E., & Gunter-Hunt, G. (1983). Simulated site visits in the relocation of older people. *Health & Social Work*, 8(1), 5–14; Markus, E., Blenkner, M., Bloom, M., & Downs, T. (1971). The impact of relocation upon mortality rates of institutionalized aged persons. *Journal of Gerontology*, 26(4), 537–538; Killian, E.C. (1970). The effects of geriatric transfer on mortality rates. *Social Work*, 15(1), 19–26.

15. National Association of Medicaid Fraud Control Units (NAMFCU). (2019). Medicaid Fraud Control Units. Retrieved from https://www.namfcu.net/mfcu-information.php

16. Kaplan, M., & Cabral, R. (1980). Relocation trauma counseling for the elderly: A demonstration project. *Journal of Gerontological Social Work*, 22(4), 321–329.

Substance Abuse

ALCOHOL AND DRUG ABUSE among older adults, particularly prescription drug abuse, is one of the fastest-growing health problems facing our society. According to the National Council on Alcohol and Drug Dependence, up to 11% of hospital admissions of older adults are because of drug- and alcohol-related issues.[1] The rate at which older adults are admitted to psychiatric hospitals for alcohol or drug abuse is 20%. Given the higher prevalence of comorbid medical problems, older adults are at higher risk for medical consequences associated with substance abuse.

Alcohol Abuse

It is estimated that nearly 50% of residents in long-term care settings and assisted living facilities have alcohol-related problems.[1] Older adults experience the effects of alcohol more quickly than younger people. They generally have less muscle mass to absorb the alcohol, causing more alcohol to flow through the bloodstream. This results in the effects lasting for longer periods of time until the alcohol is completely absorbed, as well as a higher blood alcohol concentration (BAC) level, which indicates the level of intoxication. This low tolerance for alcohol, combined with limited mobility and poor balance, puts older adults at higher risk for falls, car accidents, and other injuries. There is also consensus that alcohol contributes to cognitive deficits in older adults.[1]

Although binge drinking is often associated with young adults, it is estimated that 1 in 10 older adults is considered a binge drinker.[2] By definition, binge drinking means drinking to the point of intoxication, usually by consuming five or more alcoholic drinks at a time. A 2019 study published in the *Journal of the American Geriatrics Society* found that among older adults, binge drinking is more prevalent in men, people who currently use tobacco and/or marijuana, African Americans, and persons with lower education levels (i.e., high school or less). In addition to increasing the risk of falls, other accidents, blackouts, cognitive impairment, depression, and suicide in older adults, binge drinking even infrequently may negatively affect other health conditions by exacerbating disease, interacting with prescribed medications, and complicating disease management.[2]

Drug Abuse

People aged 65 and older use almost 30% of all prescribed medications in the United States.[3] One-quarter of the prescription drugs sold are used by older adults, and the prevalence of abuse may be as high as 11%.[4] Common prescription drugs with potential for abuse include those for anxiety, pain, and insomnia, such as benzodiazepines, opiate analgesics, and skeletal muscle relaxants. In addition to prescription medications, many older adults also use over-the-counter (OTC) medicines and dietary supplements.

Aging makes individuals more vulnerable to drug effects and interactions. Products containing alcohol or caffeine as well as cold and allergy remedies with anticholinergic antihistamines are problematic for older adults. Sedatives and hypnotics, narcotic analgesics, and nonsteroidal anti-inflammatory agents can impair cognition, jeopardize the liver or kidneys, or erode the stomach when misused.

Opioid Use

The United States is currently in the midst of an opioid epidemic. Although opioid use is more common in younger persons, the prevalence of opioid abuse among older adults is also growing. Opioid misuse poses unique risks in the geriatric population. From 1996 through 2010, the number of opioid prescriptions provided to older patients increased nine-fold. More alarming, 35% of patients aged 50 and older with chronic pain reported misuse of their opioid prescription.[5] The hospitalization rate for geriatric misuse of opioids has quintupled in the past 20 years.[6]

The evaluation of pain and the subsequent issue of pain control challenge today's healthcare providers. Treating pain in the older adult is especially difficult given the many physiological, pharmacological, and psychological complexities of caring for the geriatric patient. Healthcare professionals must carefully monitor the efficacy and side effects of opioids when used in a population with impaired metabolism, excretion, and physical reserve. Common issues to consider with opioid use in the older adult include polypharmacy, multiple comorbidities, and the potential for more side effects. During the early years of my geriatric social work practice, I did not encounter many older clients with opioid addictions. It was in the last year of my practice that I met Linda.

Linda was a new resident at the senior adult community, and her daughter had asked me to see her. When I first entered Linda's apartment, I was overwhelmed by the strong odor of cigarette smoke. Linda was a chain smoker and smoked continually throughout our sessions. I soon learned that smoking wasn't Linda's only addiction.

Although she appeared younger than her 75 years, Linda was very thin, and when I questioned her about her nutrition, she confessed that she had an eating disorder. During our weekly sessions, it also became evident that Linda was addicted to opioids. She reported that her use of opioids began following shoulder surgery, which resulted in chronic pain. When she moved to be closer to her daughter, her family realized the seriousness of her addiction and encouraged her to seek help. Linda located a physician in her new community who was willing to continue prescribing opioids. Although she was no longer driving, she would hire a cab to take her to the clinic every month to get her drugs. Despite several months of counseling and attempts to encourage Linda to participate in addiction recovery groups, she refused to deal with her addiction and ended our counseling sessions.

Marijuana Use

With the recent legalization of medical and recreational marijuana in several states, researchers are beginning to look at marijuana use by older adults. In the United States, people aged 65 and older are among the fastest-growing group of cannabis users. To date, medical marijuana has been legalized in 33 states and the District of Columbia.[7] There is increasing evidence that medical marijuana may reduce opioid use in older adults. A recent study shows that up to 65% of older adults who used medical marijuana significantly reduced their chronic pain and dependence on opioid painkillers.[8]

Indications for medical cannabis need to be weighed against side effects, to which older adults may be more vulnerable. The use of medical cannabis in this population has helped to relieve chronic pain, sleep problems, neuropathy, and anxiety. Adverse effects, such as sleepiness, balance problems, and gastrointestinal disturbances, have been experienced in a small number of patients, with some problems being resolved when dosages were adjusted.

Identifying Substance Abuse in Older Adults

Substance abuse problems are often misdiagnosed in older adults. Perhaps as a result of ageism or generational stereotyping, the topic of substance abuse and dependence is rarely associated with older adults, yet clinical research is beginning to identify the consequences of unrecognized substance abuse in the aging population. Complications that frequently occur with age, such as medical comorbidity, cognitive impairment, and frailty, contribute to the adverse interactions between substance abuse or misuse and an aging brain.

Signs that may indicate a drinking or drug problem in an older adult include the following:

- Solitary or secretive drinking
- A loss of interest in hobbies or pleasurable activities
- Drinking with disregard for warning labels on prescription drugs
- Frequent use of tranquilizers
- Slurred speech
- Presence of empty liquor and beer bottles
- Smell of alcohol on breath

- Changes in personal appearance
- Chronic and unsupported health complaints
- Hostility or depression
- Memory loss and confusion

Symptoms of alcohol withdrawal in older adults are often missed and are easily attributed to a cause other than alcohol abuse. Alcohol withdrawal disorders include tremulous syndrome, hallucinations, seizures, and delirium tremens.

A challenge to diagnosing substance abuse is the denial of this health problem by older adults. In addition to a clinical interview, a comprehensive evaluation should include a medical evaluation; laboratory analysis; and psychiatric, neurological, and social evaluations. Several screening instruments are effective for detecting substance abuse in older adults (e.g., the CAGE questionnaire, the Alcohol Use Disorders Identification Test, the Michigan Alcoholism Screening Test–Geriatric Version [MAST-G]).[9]

Older adults with substance abuse problems can be categorized as early-onset or late-onset abusers. In early-onset abusers, substance abuse develops before age 65. In these individuals, the incidence of psychiatric and physical problems tends to be higher than in late-onset abusers. In late-onset substance abuse, the abuse of drugs and/or alcohol is often thought to develop in response to stressful life situations, such as the losses that commonly occur with aging (e.g., death of a spouse or partner, changes in living situation, retirement, and social isolation). These individuals typically experience fewer physical and mental health problems than early-onset abusers.[10]

Treatment of Substance Abuse in Older Adults

The choice of treatment for substance abuse depends on the severity of the condition and the level of functional impairment and varies from hospitalization to outpatient care. The need for detoxification and the potential for serious withdrawal symptoms should be carefully evaluated.

It is important to understand ways to engage the older adult in substance abuse treatment. Psychoeducation about excessive alcohol use and the risks associated with combining alcohol with medications has proven to be effective in some cases. Clinical research has shown that approximately 10%–30% of problem drinkers have been able to reduce their drinking following one to three brief intervention sessions.[11]

Motivational interviewing has been validated as an effective treatment and motivator for change. Cognitive behavioral therapy is also frequently used in the treatment of substance abuse. Participation in Alcoholics Anonymous (AA) meetings can also be an important part of a treatment plan. Meetings that have an age-matched cohort provide mutual support, allow for peer bonding, and foster the development of peer–sobriety support networks.

Psychopharmacological treatment for substance abuse should be used with caution in older adults because of the increased risk of respiratory suppression, sedation, delirium, and other serious adverse effects. In substance abuse treatment, the social worker's willingness to educate the older client without being punitive should be coupled with realistic optimism for the future. This approach offers the best hope for recovery and reduction of the personal and social costs of substance abuse for older adults.

CHAPTER NOTES

1. National Council on Alcoholism and Drug Dependence. (2017). *Alcohol, drug dependence and seniors.* New York: National Council on Alcoholism and Drug Dependence.
2. Han, B.H., Moore, A.A., Ferris, R., & Palamar, J.J. (2019). Binge drinking among older adults in the United States, 2015–2017. *Journal of the American Geriatrics Society, 67*(7), 1–6.
3. Substance Abuse and Mental Health Services Administration. (2010). *Results from the 2009 National Survey on Drug Use and Health: Volume I. Summary of national findings* (Office of Applied Studies, NSDUH Series H-38A, HHS Publication No. SMA 10-4586 Findings). Rockville, MD: SAMHSA.
4. Brennan, P.L., & Moos, R.H. (1996). Late-life drinking behavior: The influence of personal characteristics, life context, and treatment. *Alcohol Health & Research World, 20*(3), 197–204.
5. West, N.A., Severtson, S.G., Green, J.L., & Dart, R.C. (2015). Trends in abuse and misuse of prescription opioids among older adults. *Drug and Alcohol Dependence, 1,* 117–121. doi:10.1016/j.drugalcdep.2015.01.027
6. Owens, P.L., Barrett, M.L., Weiss, A.J., Washington, R.E., & Kronick, R. (2014). *Hospital inpatient utilization related to opioid overuse among adults, 1993-2012* (HCUP Statistical Brief #177). Rockville, MD: Agency for Healthcare Research and Quality. Retrieved from http://www.hcup-us.ahrq.gov/reports/statbriefs/sb177 -Hospitalizations-for-Opioid-Overuse.pdf
7. Bargnes, V., Hart, P., Gupta, S., & Mechtler, L. (2019). Safety and efficacy of medical cannabis in elderly patients: A retrospective review in a neurological outpatient setting. *Neurology, 92* (15 Supplement), P4.1-014. Retrieved from https://n .neurology.org/content/92/15_Supplement/P4.1-014

8. Northwell Health. (2018, May 1). Medical marijuana could reduce opioid use in older adults: Study shows up to 65 percent of older adults who use medical marijuana significantly reduced their chronic pain and dependence on opioid painkillers. *ScienceDaily*. Retrieved from https://www.sciencedaily.com/releases /2018/05/180501085137.htm

9. Moore, A.A., Seeman, T., Morgenstern, H., Beck, J.C., & Reuben, D.B. (2002). Are there differences between older persons who screen positive on the CAGE questionnaire and the Short Michigan Alcoholism Screening Test-Geriatric Version? *Journal of the American Geriatrics Society, 50*(5), 858–886.

10. George, L.K., Landerman, R., Blazer, D.G., et al. (1991). Cognitive impairment. In L.N. Robins & D.A. Regier (Eds.), *Psychiatric disorders in America: The Epidemiologic Catchment Area Study* (pp. 291–327). New York: Free Press.

11. Fleming, M.F., Manwell, L.B., Barry, K.L., Adams, W., & Stauffacher, E.A. (1999). Brief physician advice for alcohol problems in older adults: A randomized community-based trial. *The Journal of Family Practice, 48*(5), 378–384.

Geriatric Social Work: Settings and Opportunities

Social workers provide services to older adults and their families in many settings. They work with older people who are healthy and active as well as those who are in poor health. Through direct services, program development, community development, training, research, and advocacy, social workers help older adults achieve and maintain a better quality of life. Geriatric social work is among the fastest-growing career fields. It is rewarding work, with many possibilities for making a difference in the lives of older adults and their families. The following chapters describe various opportunities in geriatric social work and the many meaningful roles that social workers assume when working with older adults in a range of settings.

CHAPTER 12

Medical Settings

KEY POINTS

- The care of geriatric patients in healthcare settings is structured using the interdisciplinary team model.

- Medical social workers play an important role in identifying and responding to elder abuse in the hospital setting.

- Social workers in healthcare settings help identify unmet needs in geriatric patients and assist them in navigating the complex healthcare system.

IN THE MEDICAL FIELD, geriatric patients commonly present with health problems that are both complex and chronic. Chronic health problems, such as cardiovascular complaints, arthritis, or a decline in pulmonary function, are more typical in older patients than in younger ones. The complexity of health problems faced by older adults stems from several factors:

- Geriatric patients may have multiple health issues, each affecting the others.

- Problems may present differently in geriatric patients than in younger patients.

- Geriatric patients are likely to present inconsistent information about their health concerns.

- Current health problems are influenced by a lengthy history of medical and psychosocial problems in older patients.

- Older patients bring complex attitudes toward healthcare based on their past involvement with other healthcare providers.

Because of these issues, care of geriatric patients in healthcare settings is typically structured using the interdisciplinary team model.[1] For most social workers in healthcare settings, this means being prepared to work as a member of this interdisciplinary team. Knowledge of other professionals, what their roles are, and the language and terminology they use is essential to the development of team relationships. Skills that are necessary for all team members include knowledge and respect for other team members' abilities; the ability to conceptualize cases holistically; the expertise to develop team treatment plans and communication, leadership, and conflict resolution skills; and the ability to anticipate and respond to change.

Interdisciplinary teams are composed of members of several disciplines who use their professional knowledge to generate a plan of care through collaboration and consensus decision-making. All team members are assumed to be colleagues, and there is no hierarchical team organization. Leadership functions are shared among members. The group as a whole is responsible for program effectiveness and team function.

Education Programs for Social Work in Healthcare Settings

One of the earliest interdisciplinary team-training programs was developed by the Department of Veterans Affairs (VA).[2,3] Conducted in clinical education settings at twelve VA medical centers across the United States, the program began in the late 1970s and early 1980s with a major initiative to develop integrated primary and specialty care for geriatric veterans. Since then, social work schools have begun to offer programs on social work in healthcare settings that focus on interdisciplinary training.[4]

Arizona State University's School of Social Work offers interdisciplinary training that brings social work students together with students from the university's schools of medicine, pharmacy, nursing, and nutrition. The program's focus is on clinical training sites and includes online learning modules, simulation exercises, and student internships that promote interprofessional collaboration. The University of Texas at Austin's Steve Hicks School of Social Work has always incorporated interdisciplinary training that includes medical and nursing students and has more recently added pharmacy students to the program as well as training opportunities with the law school. The University of Iowa School of Social Work's distance learning program is unique in its affiliation with the National Coalition Building Institute, an organization that provides training in diversity, equity, and inclusion in community organizations, schools, colleges and university campuses, corporations, and law enforcement. Students are required to take a course through the Institute that builds an atmosphere in which they can learn to work on interdisciplinary teams.

Hospitals

As people age and their health declines, they may require hospitalization for medical or surgical treatment. While these individuals are hospitalized, it is not uncommon for existing mental health disorders to also be identified and treated. In addition, new symptoms of mental health disturbances, such as depression or anxiety, may develop in relation to the patient's medical condition or hospitalization. As a result, many older adults in a hospital setting receive some type of psychiatric medication that is often provided by clinicians who are not psychiatrists.

In addition to assisting older adults with mental health conditions, social workers in hospital settings also play an important role in identifying and responding to elder abuse. Because visits to the emergency room may be the only time an older adult leaves his or her home, emergency room staff can be a first line of defense in identifying abuse victims. The most common kinds of elder abuse are emotional, physical, and financial (see Table 8.1), and usually when one type of abuse exists, there are other forms also present. Social workers are often available on call to respond to signs of elder abuse that are identified in emergency settings and to work with other members of the healthcare team to begin an investigation.

To make awareness of elder abuse part of the culture in emergency settings, all staff need to be trained. Unlike cases of child abuse, in which there is a standard protocol in place for screening, only recently has an equivalent protocol for older victims of abuse emerged. A comprehensive protocol begins with an interview and head-to-toe physical exam that looks for bruises, lacerations, abrasions, and areas of pain and tenderness. Additional testing is ordered if abuse is suspected. The healthcare team looks for specific injuries. For example, X rays may show old and new fractures, which suggest a pattern of multiple traumatic events. Specific types of fractures might indicate abuse, such as midshaft fractures in the ulna, a forearm bone that can break when an older adult holds his or her arm in front of the face in self-protection. Another red flag for possible abuse or neglect is a record of frequent emergency room visits.

When signs of elder abuse are found but the older patient refuses help or a safer living arrangement, it may be necessary to determine if the individual has decision-making capacity (see Chapter 7). Patients who are in immediate danger and want help or are found not to have capacity may be admitted to the hospital until the social worker can work on a safe discharge plan. For at-risk patients who have been determined to have decision-making capacity and are refusing assistance, a referral to Adult Protective Services for follow-up should be made. In this chapter, I recap my history of experiences working in hospital settings, an exciting career path that involved protecting the welfare of older adults, tending to the psychosocial needs of geriatric patients, developing a hospital-based eldercare program, and helping social work gain recognition as an important part of the medical team.

One of the advantages of getting older and sometimes wiser is the opportunity to look back and appreciate events that took us in directions that we would have never considered in our life plans. When I entered graduate school, several of the community organization courses that I had planned to take were no longer being offered, so I made the life-altering decision to take my electives in medical social work. Taught by a former chief of social work at the VA who had served as the head of the National Association for Hospital Social Work Directors, these courses gave me the skills necessary to administer several hospital social work departments throughout my career.

Shortly after I obtained my M.S.W. degree, I was offered a social work position in a hospital setting. Built in 1884 by the Sisters of Charity, Sheehan Emergency Hospital (later renamed Sheehan Memorial Hospital) in Buffalo, New York, was a small Catholic hospital located on the east side of the city.[5] In addition to providing general and acute patient care, it also served as the burn treatment center for western New York. As I drove through the neighborhood on the way to my interview, it was hard not to notice the boarded storefronts and deserted streets. The hospital building was old with obvious signs of neglect. When I pulled up to the front, I was instructed to park in the lot next to the building, which was fenced, with a security guard stationed at the entrance.

The interior of the building was dismal, with peeling paint on the walls and outdated furnishings throughout. Patient areas consisted of wards, some with as many as eight beds lining the walls. The burn unit was a startling contrast to the rest of the hospital environment, with brightly painted walls and modern furniture in the waiting room. Although I was unable to go inside the patient care area because it was an isolation unit, I was able to get a glimpse of this modern, well-equipped unit through a window.

Despite the hospital's appearance and its location in a high-crime neighborhood, I saw an opportunity to provide social work services to a patient population with many medical, economic, and social needs. As a nonprofit Catholic hospital, Sheehan did not have the funding to support a large staff or pay high wages, but I was told by the hospital's administrator that construction was underway to build a new facility nearby, and that plans included adding additional social work staff.

My job responsibilities included managing the hospital's social work department, which consisted of a secretary and me, and providing social work services to patients. Most of the patients came from nearby neighborhoods, which were predominately African American and Polish. The hospital did not have obstetric or pediatric departments—those patients were admitted to one of the other hospitals in the Buffalo area. It was not unusual for Sheehan's census to include several patients who had been in the hospital for several months awaiting placement. This situation was not unique to Sheehan, but was a common problem faced by other hospitals in the region as well. That year, it was estimated that over 800 patients in western New York hospitals were awaiting placement, with some hospitalized for over a year. Because most of our patients were low-income or below the poverty line, discharge planning was difficult, as they lacked sufficient resources to qualify for alternative living arrangements. For some patients, discharge back to their home placed them at risk of harm from unsafe living conditions or fraud, neglect, or abuse by family members. Maddie was one such patient.

I received a call from the nursing station informing me that a patient in need of social work services had just been admitted. In the few months that I had been working at the hospital, I had seen an increase in the number of referrals by hospital staff.

By building relationships and educating staff about the role of the social worker on the healthcare team, I had demonstrated the value of social work and how it made their jobs easier.

The patient, Maddie, was lying in her bed when I entered the room. In a small, weak voice, she greeted me and explained that she had been brought to the hospital because she wasn't eating. After reading her chart and talking to her nurse, I learned that this 90-year-old woman had been admitted to the hospital after police responded to a call from her neighbor, who was concerned that she hadn't left her home in days. Entering the house, police found Maddie lying in a urine-soaked bed, its headboard holding up the wall behind it. There were empty saltine cracker wrappers scattered on the bed and the floor. The police report stated that the conditions in the home were unsafe and that there was garbage scattered throughout. The small amount of food that was found in the refrigerator was spoiled.

Maddie was not found to be suffering from any acute medical condition but was diagnosed with malnutrition. The members of her treatment team recommended that she not return to her unsafe environment but instead be discharged to a nursing home. My attempts to involve her family in the discharge plan were unsuccessful. In fact, the family did not respond to my calls or visit Maddie at the hospital. I placed Maddie on the waiting lists of the nursing homes that accepted indigent patients, her name yet another to add to the long list of patients awaiting a nursing home bed.

Several weeks later, I received a call from a man who identified himself as Maddie's grandson. "I just found out that my grandmother is in the hospital, and I want to take her to live with me," he told me. There was something in his voice and manner that caused me to question his sincerity and intent, especially after the lack of interest and involvement shown by Maddie's family in the weeks since she had been hospitalized. But when I told Maddie that her grandson wanted to take care of her, a big grin spread across her face, and she became very excited.

Still uneasy about Maddie's new discharge plan, I checked with the hospital's admitting office to determine if she had any money or other items with her when she was admitted.

In addition to a small wallet with Social Security and Medicare cards, there was a bank book that showed a balance of $600. Maddie was legally competent to make decisions about her care, but as her social worker, I was bound by my professional ethics to report any concerns I had about her welfare. I contacted Adult Protective Services, and it was discovered that Maddie's grandson had a police record that included several charges of credit card fraud. However, because there was no evidence that any crime had been committed against Maddie, it was decided that she would still be discharged into her grandson's care, with follow-up by Adult Protective Services.

When Maddie's grandson arrived at the hospital on the day of her discharge, he was instructed to come to my office, where I gave him information about home care services. The police had been alerted and were ready to come in if needed. My secretary was in the adjoining office and was instructed to call them if she thought that I was in any danger. After leaving my office, Maddie and her grandson stopped at the admitting office, where her bank book was given to her grandson. One hour later, I received a phone call from the police. After leaving the hospital, Maddie's grandson drove straight to the bank and attempted to withdraw all her money. Having been alerted by the police prior to his arrival, the bank called them, and he was arrested. Confused and saddened by her grandson's behavior, Maddie was brought back to the hospital, where she remained until she was transferred to a nursing home.

As the social worker for the burn unit at Sheehan, I was a member of the burn treatment team and participated in patient rounds once a week. Although I was comfortable working in medical settings, I was unprepared for the acute pain, suffering, and disfigurement that I would witness in the burn unit. Burn patients represent the most severe model of trauma, and the complexity of the treatment of severe burn injuries led to the development of regional burn centers. As the designated burn treatment center for western New York, Sheehan admitted the most serious burn victims in the region, except for children. Those patients were sent to the pediatric burn treatment unit in Rochester, New York.

My work with burn patients was very different from my other experiences as a hospital social worker. In order to enter the unit to talk to my patients, I had to don the clothing that was required for all treatment team members who work in an isolation unit. Although burn patients are not usually contagious, they are highly susceptible to infections. A sterile gown, head covering, and booties had to be put on before entering the unit. The treatment team was composed of physicians, nurses, occupational and physical therapists, a dietitian, and a social worker. Unlike my caseload in the other areas of the hospital, I was expected to see every patient on the burn unit rather than wait for a referral from other hospital staff. The mental state of the burn patient has an important impact on care, with aspects such as pain tolerance, anxiety level, and motivation all critical to recovery. Medical advances in the treatment of patients following severe burn injuries have significantly improved their survival rate and prognosis, but the adjustment to major burns is a prolonged and difficult journey for patients and their families.[6]

Medical social work in a hospital setting often involves crisis counseling, particularly in the emergency room and in other departments that provide trauma care. In the burn unit, I was available to help patients and their families through the initial crisis. Once the patient's condition stabilized, I assessed his or her ongoing needs, provided counseling, suggested appropriate services, and addressed problems or concerns that arose during hospitalization. For many patients with severe burns, counseling to help deal with disfigurement and the loss of facial and body image was important. Working with the other members of the care team, I facilitated the patient's release from the hospital, referring the patient and his or her family members for community resources.

Crisis and bereavement counseling was also provided to families of burn patients who did not survive. The survival rate for geriatric burn patients was poor, particularly for those who had burns over 30 percent or more of their body. The comorbid factors responsible for this increase in morbidity and mortality were thin skin, decreased pulmonary reserves, poor circulation, malnutrition, and increased susceptibility to infection. These factors contribute to a rate of burn shock, inhalation injury, pulmonary pathology, septicemia, and renal failure that is higher than in younger people. Many of the older burn patients were victims of house fires or accidents in their homes, particularly in the kitchen and bathroom.[7]

In 1980, I relocated to Florida, where I accepted a position as a medical social worker at Indian River Memorial Hospital in Vero Beach, a small retirement community on the Atlantic Ocean. The contrast between Indian River and Sheehan could not have been greater.

A community nonprofit hospital, Indian River was situated on a large green plot of land just north of Vero Beach and was surrounded by orange groves. The building was modern and well-kept. All 240 patient rooms were private. Unlike Sheehan, this hospital had obstetric and pediatric departments. The social work department consisted of a director, one B.S.W social worker, and the hospital patient-relations coordinator.

As I stepped into the hospital elevator on my first day, I was greeted by one of the physicians, who introduced himself and asked me who I was. When I informed him that I was a social worker, I was unprepared for his response. "Why, where I come from, we eat social workers for breakfast," he responded with a smile. Although most of the hospital's medical staff regarded social workers as important members of the team, I soon learned that some professionals had never worked with social workers and did not see the need for their involvement in patient care. This was more true in healthcare settings in the rural South—a stark contrast to my experiences in the Northeast.

Nevertheless, Indian River's social work department continued to grow, with the addition of another social worker assigned to the intensive care and coronary care units and a mental health therapist who covered the obstetric and pediatric units. Six months after I started working at the hospital, the social work director was terminated and I was appointed the department director. My transition was an easy one, with the help of a supportive staff as well as the support and cooperation shown by other hospital personnel. My previous experience as a department director in Buffalo was an asset. I also silently expressed words of gratitude to the professor of my medical social work class at Catholic University each time I had to prepare a budget, develop department policies and procedures, or prepare for a Joint Commission on Accreditation (JCAHO) survey.[8]

Under the previous director, the social work department at Indian River had suffered from poor staff morale and the lack of a strong presence in the hospital. My first task was to rebuild relationships. In the weeks following my promotion, I scheduled meetings with other hospital departments to discuss how social work could address the emotional and social components of healthcare and contribute to the hospital's overall goal of high-quality patient care.

As the social work department's visibility and reputation grew, so did the participation of our staff on hospital care teams and committees.

I became a member of the hospital's Utilization Review Committee, which allowed me to play a role in the monitoring and improvement of patient care. As with most hospitals during that time period, discharge planning at Indian River was a primary function of the social work department. To facilitate a successful discharge plan, it was essential to establish and nurture strong working relationships with the service providers and agencies in the community. All social work staff were encouraged to participate in community service, most often by serving on agency boards and committees.

To improve the coordination of discharge planning for the hospital's large number of older patients, I established and chaired a multidisciplinary discharge planning committee. Members of the committee included the directors of the physical and occupational therapy departments as well as representatives from social work, nursing, dietary, and other rehabilitation departments. Physicians were invited but rarely attended. The committee met weekly to discuss and coordinate discharge plans for patients who had been identified as needing post-hospital care.

To improve morale among the social work staff, I instituted a weekly staff meeting, which provided the opportunity to discuss difficult cases. Information about hospital events and employee and policy changes was also shared with the staff at these meetings. Florida had recently passed legislation that established state licensure for mental health professionals. I began the process of becoming a Licensed Clinical Social Worker (LCSW) and urged those staff members who were eligible to also become licensed.

Before making any changes in staffing, I reviewed the social work caseload to determine the number and types of referrals received and the services that were provided. Then, I looked at hospital admissions. Most of the patient population came from Vero Beach, where 23% of the population was aged 65 and older. These numbers did not include the "snowbirds" who spent the winter months on Vero's beaches. The advanced age of many of our admissions and the fact that few had family living in the area were important factors in determining post-hospital needs. I found that at least 40% of the hospital's admissions required social work services. The numbers included pediatric and obstetrical patients. Social work staff were assigned to patient care areas based on their expertise and interest in working with that patient population. They were encouraged to become a member of their designated patient care team and to attend unit meetings and social events. Staff coverage for the emergency room as well as evening and weekend on-call was rotated on a weekly basis.

As a department director, I reported directly to the hospital administrator, which was an advantage when it came to making policy changes and obtaining resources for the department. One notable change implemented was that a social worker no longer had to wait for a physician referral to see a patient. Every morning, I would scan the new admissions, screening for risk factors such as diagnosis, age, admission from a nursing home, or a recent history of readmissions. Those patients determined to be at high risk were assigned to a social worker to be assessed. Many referrals were now coming from other members of the patient care team, including nurses, rehabilitation therapists, and dieticians. The increase in the number of referrals for social work services made it necessary to add two additional social workers to the staff. A B.S.W. student intern from a nearby university also joined the department and was hired upon graduation.

As my staff and I continued to build professional relationships within the hospital and in the community, we demonstrated the value of social work in patient care and were able to build a cohesive and highly respected social work department. Medical social work had become an integral component of patient care in most hospitals throughout the country, but except for the state's large medical centers and teaching hospitals, it was still not embraced by many Florida hospitals. Since moving from New York, I had continued my memberships in national professional organizations, presenting at conferences and attending workshops. One of the organizations, The Society of Hospital Social Work Directors, had several chapters in Florida, and I became active in the Southeast District Chapter, eventually serving as chairperson.[9]

The increasing number of geriatric admissions led the hospital to develop an ongoing hospital-based eldercare program. As chair of the hospital's eldercare task force committee, I used my knowledge and experience in geriatric care to help develop a program for people in the community aged 55 and older and their caregivers. The name of the program, "REGARD," was chosen to convey concern, consideration, respect, affection, and esteem for older adults in the community. There were six services provided, along with a quarterly newsletter. These services included a community resource helpline, a Medicare-assistance line, weekly wellness walks, a series of caregiver-education presentations, a caregiver fair, and a respite service that provided a weekend stay in a designated area of the hospital for older adults whose caregivers needed a break from their caregiving responsibilities. Hospital volunteers were trained to staff the respite program, providing supervision and activities for the participants.

In March of 1985, I was selected as "Social Worker of the Year" by the Gulfstream Unit of the National Association of Social Workers Florida Chapter. The award was given in recognition of my efforts to develop comprehensive and high-quality social work services in a hospital set-ting, with a certification that stated, "Her unit has distinguished itself for its professionalism and growth over the last few years." It was an honor to be recognized by my fellow social workers, especially because the nomi-nation for the award came from one of the social workers on my staff.

————————————————

Home Health Services

The centerpiece of the healthcare delivery system, home health services involve a formal, regulated program of care in which various medical, therapeutic, and nonmedical services are delivered by healthcare profes-sionals in the person's home. The majority (70%) of home health patients are 65 and older, with more than one million of them receiving home health services each day.[10] Home health services play an integral role in managing and treating many symptoms of chronic and acute health conditions, especially those that are most prevalent with aging, such as hypertension, arthritis, heart disease, cancer, diabetes, and stroke.

Home care offers several advantages. Healthcare in a home setting may be more cost-effective than treatment provided in a hospital, and it may reduce exposure to healthcare-associated infections. Healthcare pro-vided in an individual's home also supports aging in place and indepen-dence, important factors in maintaining a high quality of life for older adults. Many geriatric social workers help provide home health services so that older adults can remain at home for as long as possible.

The Prospective Payment System (PPS), implemented in 2000,[11] was instrumental in social work becoming a part of home health service delivery. The PPS for Medicare-funded home health services changed the 35-year history of reimbursing home health agencies on a fee-for-service basis to a flat rate reimbursement for each patient. As a result, the focus on how services are provided shifted from service output to service outcomes. These changes required coordination and collaboration among all members of the home health team and presented an opportunity for social workers to offer much-needed psychosocial services to geriatric patients.

Medicare requires every home health agency to offer social work services, but there is no requirement that social workers see all patients or participate in planning their care. Home health social work services are not considered primary services like skilled nursing, physical therapy, and speech therapy, making it necessary for social workers to receive a referral from a nurse or other primary service provider before seeing a patient. The key to justifying reimbursement of skilled social work services is to identify social and emotional problems impacting the patient's medical condition, treatment plan, or rate of recovery. A social work treatment plan can then be developed to address these issues.

Home health social workers view their patients from an environmental or a family systems perspective. They provide direct patient services, such as psychosocial assessment, counseling for patients and family members, crisis intervention, and short-term therapy. They also provide patient education and placement services for patients after discharge from home health services. Coordinating services, completing applications for government benefits, and collaborating with other professionals are other common responsibilities for social workers involved in home care. Newer roles for home health social workers include providing caregiver support services and working with managed care organizations.

Hospice

Approximately 90 million Americans are living with serious and life-threatening illnesses, a number that is expected to double over the next 20 years with the aging of the baby boomers.[12] Most serious chronic illnesses occur in those aged 65 and older. These older adults often live with and die from chronic illnesses that are preceded by long periods of physical decline and functional impairment.

Although related, hospice and palliative care are different in several ways. Hospice care is offered to patients with an acute terminal illness who have less than 6 months to live. Palliative care is medical treatment provided to help patients manage the symptoms of their condition rather than to cure a disease. Hospice care includes palliative care, but palliative care may also be provided to patients without terminal illnesses. Palliative care offers an approach that is well-suited for older adults.

By relieving symptoms of pain and the stress of serious illnesses, palliative care improves the quality of life for older adults. Through its multidisciplinary, holistic approach, the "boomerang" experience of crisis-hospitalization-rehab-readmit-crisis cycles that cause distress and suffering for geriatric patients can often be prevented.[13]

Hospice care and palliative care are provided not only at inpatient hospice centers but also in palliative care programs at hospitals and through in-home services. In these settings, medical care is provided with an emphasis on pain management, emotional support for patients and their families, and resource-navigation services. Hospice and palliative care social workers typically work as members of an interdisciplinary team consisting of care providers that also include physicians, nurses, medical assistants, and clergy. Depending on their work setting, hospice and palliative care social workers may specialize in a specific age group, such as older adults or pediatric patients, or they may work with patients of all ages. They are available to help patients and caregivers deal with the practical and emotional challenges that occur at the end of life.[14]

Patients who require hospice care and their families experience multiple challenges that may include depression, anger, and anxiety; physical pain and discomfort; financial strain; social isolation; caregiver stress; and family conflict. Hospice social workers help patients and their families navigate the challenging process of end-of-life planning; manage the emotional, familial, and monetary stressors of debilitating illness; understand and participate in the treatment plan; and connect with other support services in the community.

People who seek medical care need guidance beyond the identification and treatment of a health problem.[14] Social workers can help identify unmet needs in geriatric patients with chronic and acute illnesses, assist them in navigating the complex healthcare system, and support them in attaining optimal levels of functioning.

CHAPTER NOTES

1. For additional reading on interdisciplinary healthcare teams, see Nancarron, S.A., Booth, A., Ariss, S., Smith, T., Enderby, P., & Roots, A. (2013). Ten principles of good interdisciplinary team work. *Human Resources for Health, 11*(19), 1–11. doi: 10.1186/1478-4491-11-19; O'Connor, M., & Fisher, C. (2011). Exploring the dynamics of interdisciplinary palliative care teams in providing psychosocial care: Everyone thinks that everybody can do it and they can't. *Journal of Palliative Medicine, 14*(2), 191–196; Wieland, D., Kramer, B.J., Waite, M.S., & Rubenstein, L.Z. (1996). The interdisciplinary team in geriatric care. *American Behavioral Scientist, 39*(6), 658–664.

2. Rasin-Waters, D., Abel, V., Kearney, L.K., & Zeiss, A. (2018). The integrated care team approach of the Department of Veterans Affairs (VA): Geriatric primary care. *Archives of Clinical Neuropsychology, 33*(3), 280–289.

3. Heinemann, G.P., & Zeiss, A.N. (Eds.) (2002). *Team performance in health care: Assessment and development.* New York: Kluwer Academic/Plenum Press.

4. Laurio, A. (2018, April). Social work education: Interdisciplinary teams a growing area of training. *NASW News.* Retrieved from https://www.socialworkers.org/News/NASW-News/ID/1635/Social-Work-Education-Interdisciplinary-teams-a-growing-area-of-training

5. Sheehan Memorial Hospital operated the Western New York region's premier burn treatment center until the mid-1980s, when the unit was transferred to the Erie County Medical Center. The hospital filed for Chapter 11 protection in 2004 but emerged from bankruptcy in 2006, focusing on drug treatment. In 2013, Sheehan Memorial Hospital closed, and the property was converted into a community health clinic and office building.

6. For further reading about social work services for burn patients, see Al-Mousani, A.M., Mecott-Rivera, G.A., Jeschke, M.G., & Herndon, D.N. (2009). Burn teams and burn centers: The importance of a comprehensive team approach to burn care. *Clinical Plastic Surgery, 36*(4), 547–554; Barrett, K. (2011). *Clinical practice guidelines: Social work (adult) burn patient management, NSW Statewide Burn Injury Service.* New South Wales, Australia: Agency for Clinical Innovation; Williams, N.R., Reeves, P.M., Cox, E.R., & Call, S.B. (2004). Creating a social work link to the burn community: A research team goes to burn camp. *Social Work in Health Care, 38*(3), 81–103; Thorton, A., & Battistel, L. (2001). Working with burn survivors: A social work approach. *Journal of Australian Social Work, 54*(3), 93–103.

7. For further reading about geriatric burn patients, see Palmieri, T.L. (2017). The elderly burn patient. In F.A. Luchette & J.A. Yelon (Eds.), *Geriatric trauma and critical care* (pp. 333–337). New York: Springer Publishing Company; Harvey, L., Mitchell, R., Brodaty, H., Draper, B., & Close, J. (2016). Dementia: A risk factor for burns in the elderly. *Burns, 42*(2), 282–290; Abu-Sittah, G.S., Chahine, F.M., & Janom, H. (2016). Management of burns in the elderly. *Annals of Burns and Fire Disasters, 29*(4), 245–249; Pham, T.N., Carrougher, G.J., Martinez, E., Lezotte, D., Rietschel, C., Holavanahalli, R., et al. (2015). Predictors of discharge disposition in older adults with burns: A study of the burn model systems. *Journal of Burn Care & Research: Official Publication of the American Burn Association, 36*(6), 607–612; Uygur, F., Noyan, N., Ülkür, E., & Çeliköz, B. (2008). A geriatric patient with major burns: Case report. *Annals of Burns and Fire Disasters, 21*(1), 43–46; Davidge, K., & Fish, J. (2008). Older adults and burns. *Geriatrics and Aging, 11*(5), 270–275; Hill, A.J., Germa, F., & Boyle, J.C. (2002). Burns in older people—Outcomes and risk factors. *Journal of the American Geriatrics Society, 50*(11),1912–1913.

8. The Joint Commission, formerly known as the Joint Commission on Accreditation of Healthcare Organizations (JCAHO), is an independent, not-for-profit organization that evaluates and accredits health care organizations in the United States and around the world. It is recognized as an indicator of quality care, and in many states, it is a condition of licensure and for the receipt of Medicare and Medicaid payments.

9. The Society of Hospital Social Work Directors was established in 1965 under the American Hospital Association. The society was brought into the federal sector in 1971. It played a role in the creation of the document *The Medicare Conditions of Participation*, published in 1986, which mandated that hospitals provide social work services and have an effective ongoing discharge planning program. In 1993, the society's name was changed to the Society for Social Work Administrators in Health Care. Four years later, the name was changed again to the Society for Social Work Leadership in Health Care to represent all social workers in leadership positions in health care settings. The society became a freestanding professional organization in 2001. See https://www.sswlhc.org.

10. Jones, A.L., Harris-Kojetin, L., & Valverde, R. (2012). *Characteristics and use of home health care by men and women aged 65 and over* (National Health Statistics Reports, Number 52). Washington, DC: The U.S. Department of Health and Human Services, Centers for Disease Control and Prevention, National Center for Health Statistics. Retrieved from https://www.cdc.gov/nchs/data/nhsr/nhsr052.pdf

11. Lee, J.S., & Rock, B.D. (2005). Challenges in the new prospective payment system: Action steps for social work in home health care. *Health & Social Work, 30* (1), 48–55.

12. Hallowell, N. (2014). End-of-life palliative care. *Today's Geriatric Medicine, 7*(5), 16.

13. For further reading about social work in hospice and palliative care settings, see NASW Center for Workforce Studies & Social Work Practice. (2010). *Social workers in hospice and palliative care: Occupation profile.* Washington, DC: The National Association of Social Workers. Retrieved from https://www.socialworkers.org/LinkClick.aspx?fileticket=rq8DPC0g-AM%3D&portalid=0; Reese, D.J. (2013). *Hospice social work.* New York: Columbia University Press; Go-Coloma, R. (2018). The role of social workers in end-of-life care. *Today's Geriatric Medicine, 11*(6), 30–32.

14. Volland, P.J. (1996). Social work practice in health care: Looking to the future with a different lens. *Social Work in Health Care, 24*(1–2), 35–51.

CHAPTER 13

Long-Term Care

KEY POINTS

- Long-term care environments range from nursing homes or assisted living facilities to housing that provides congregate facilities or services.

- A variety of factors, such as ethnicity, culture, or previous healthcare experiences, can affect an older adult's transition to a long-term care setting.

- Dementia care environments strive to offer a safe, secure, and stress-free environment for persons with Alzheimer's disease or a related disorder.

A RELATIVELY SMALL NUMBER (1.5 million) and percentage (3.1%) of the 65-and-older population live in long-term care settings. Among these individuals, 1.2 million live in nursing homes. However, the percentage of older adults living in long-term care settings increases significantly with age, ranging from 1% for persons aged 65–74 to 3% for persons aged 75–84 and 9% for persons aged 85 and older.[1] It is estimated that 5% of persons over the age of 65 are living in a nursing home at any given point in time.[2] Most residents are women over the age of 80 with significant chronic illness, functional disability, and mental impairment.

People in need of long-term care may live in many different environments, ranging from nursing homes or assisted living facilities to some form of housing that provides congregate facilities or services. Several options have developed as alternatives for older adults who reach a point when the need for increased care and supervision is more than what can be provided at home. When skilled nursing care is not needed, individuals now have choices that include assisted living facilities, continuing care retirement communities (CCRCs), board and care homes, and adult day care. (For additional information on living environments for older adults, see Chapter 10.)

Long-term care services include healthcare and social services designed to provide assessment; treatment; rehabilitation; supportive care; and the prevention of further disability in persons with chronic physical, developmental, or cognitive impairments. The need for long-term care services is expected to increase in the United States as the population ages. As the number of individuals in need of long-term care grows, new issues related to staffing, family involvement, quality of life, the role of spirituality, end-of-life care, medical management, program development, and overall service delivery are emerging.

Social Work in Long-Term Care

The National Association of Social Workers (NASW) first established standards for social workers in long-term care in 1981. The standards identified the guiding principles of social work services in these settings. These principles are designed to provide assessment, treatment, rehabilitation, and supportive care as well as to preserve and enhance social functioning[3]:

- Services are resident and family directed.

- Residents and families should be able to easily access services provided by social workers.

- A continuum of social work services is provided during the various phases of residency (e.g., preadmission, admission, residency, discharge/transfer/death).

- Services are provided within an interdisciplinary perspective and should be integrated and coordinated with linkages between appropriate agencies and programs.

- Social workers should possess a comprehensive understanding of the characteristics of the client population, of clients' developmental stages, and of the practice setting in order to competently perform social work activities with residents and their caregivers.

- Clinical practice, community, and policy approaches should be based on the unique and changing needs of the resident population.

In the long-term care industry, value and cultural conflicts often occur between healthcare professionals and the clients they serve. The social worker should be sensitive to the cultural traditions and needs of all parties and should help facilitate better understanding of differences to improve working relationships. Older adults adjust differently to a transition to long-term care depending on a variety of factors, such as ethnicity, culture, or previous healthcare experiences. For some older adults, entrance into a long-term care setting may be a continuation of past experiences with institutional care. Some members of minority groups who do not speak English or who are less acquainted with American culture may have a more difficult transition and require extra support during the adjustment process. In many cultures, elders are treated with a great deal of respect. Social workers should be observant of residents' ethnic and cultural traditions and help other residents and staff to be tolerant and supportive.

Federal and state laws uphold and protect the dignity, autonomy, and rights of older adults in long-term care settings.[4] All residents are entitled to dignity and privacy in their care. Social workers should ensure that residents' self-determination is protected when conflicts occur with families and staff. Other important rights are related to forming and maintaining meaningful social relationships. It is important to remember that the complex social and emotional needs of adulthood do not end in old age, including the need for intimacy and the expression of sexuality.

A survey published in 2013 by the Society for Post-Acute and Long-Term Care Medicine (AMDA) showed that little progress has been made in how nursing homes deal with sexual behavior among residents. Out of 175 medical directors surveyed, just 13% reported that their long-term care residences provided staff training on sexual behavior, and only 23% of long-term care settings had a policy on intimacy and sexual behavior.[5,6] In my work as a long-term care consultant, I was asked for advice on how to address sexuality in older adults on more than one occasion, as I share in the account that follows.

While working as a medical social worker, I completed the requirements for a clinical social work license in the state of New York and accepted a part-time consultant position at a Buffalo nursing home. At that time, New York required all nursing homes to have a social worker on staff.

Those facilities that did not have a social worker with an M.S.W. were required to hire a licensed social worker to provide consultation services. In my role as a consultant, I would meet with the social worker weekly to discuss residents' social, behavioral, and family issues. Consultation and staff training were also provided to other members of the healthcare team as needed. Most often, the training was focused on helping staff deal with specific behavioral or family issues.

An issue that staff found particularly difficult to address, and one that would resurface numerous times over the years, was sexual expression among nursing home residents. It was not unusual for some residents to engage in sexual activity, such as masturbation, fondling or intimate touching with another resident, or sexual intercourse. Under New York state law, nursing home residents who were legally competent had the right to sexual expression and the right to privacy. Nursing homes were mandated to provide a room where residents could have privacy when needed. This was a right that was rarely communicated to or exercised by residents, and I never saw a violation of this right cited in a state evaluation. To comply with this regulation, most nursing homes designated space for privacy that was also used for other purposes, such as medical exams or storage.

Despite residents' right to privacy and human sexuality, difficult situations would often still arise in long-term care settings, as occurred in the following scenario:

> The residents had returned to their rooms following lunch, and several of them had settled in for an afternoon nap. The nursing aide was making her way down the hall to begin afternoon care. Approaching Helen's room, she tapped lightly on the closed door and entered. As she came toward the bed, she gasped when she realized that Helen was masturbating, pushing an object in and out of her vagina with her hand. Embarrassed, Helen quickly turned away and pulled the object, a small glass perfume bottle, from between her legs. Grabbing the bottle from Helen's hand, the aide shouted, "Shame on you, Helen!"
>
> When the social worker heard about the incident, she contacted me for advice on how to address the situation. It was decided that there should be a discussion with the aide about her inappropriate response to the resident's behavior, with suggestions for a nonjudgmental approach. The social worker then had a

private conversation with Helen, reassuring her that although masturbation is not wrong, inserting a glass object into her vagina could be dangerous. When the social worker offered to assist her in purchasing a sexual aid, Helen said no and refused to discuss it any further.

A staff in-service was conducted to emphasize that many older adults still have sexual needs and that the right to express those needs should not be belittled. For residents who were mentally competent to consent to and engage in sexual behavior with others, it was recommended that the home provide opportunities for privacy. A film that I used to initiate a dialogue among staff, "Rose by Any Name," portrays two residents who develop a relationship. When they choose to share a bed in the man's private room, the staff inform the administrator, who contacts the woman's (Rose's) daughter and threatens to discharge her if her "behavior" continues. The film then shows the couple apart, sad and lonely as they sit in their separate rooms. At the end of the film, there is a shot of the hallway. The door to Rose's room opens, and she tiptoes down the hall to see her friend.

Several weeks later, I received another call from the nursing home's social worker. Helen was once again found masturbating, this time using a pill bottle. The social worker reported that she had already addressed the situation by purchasing a vibrator for Helen and leaving it, nicely gift-wrapped, on her bedside table. A privacy sign was made available to hang on Helen's door during her afternoon nap.

The greatest obstacle for long-term care residents with social and sexual needs is a lack of understanding or support among staff. Some staff may express discomfort, judgment, or disapproval at the idea of sex between older adults, particularly those who are chronically ill, disabled, or unmarried. Staff training should emphasize that sexual activity is a basic right for all older adults. The capacity for sexual consent must be assessed in those with cognitive impairment to provide protection from nonconsensual sexual aggression. Films and case examples can be used to demonstrate strategies for dealing with delicate situations.

Dementia Care

Meeting the needs of a person with Alzheimer's disease or a related disorder can become overwhelming for a family. When the need for increased care and supervision becomes more than what can be provided at home, families usually consider long-term care. Most persons with dementia do not require nursing care but rather a safe, secure, and stress-free environment. Prior to the establishment of assisted living, nursing homes were the only care settings available for older adults. Most nursing homes would not accept persons with dementia because they were unable to provide a secured environment or trained staff equipped to handle behaviors associated with the diagnosis. With the increase in the number of persons with dementia, some nursing homes began to open dementia care units. Because Medicare does not cover unskilled nursing care, these units admitted only private-pay residents. It wasn't long before long-term care companies began to realize the market for dementia care and opened assisted living dementia care programs—some remodeling a building section and others building a free-standing dementia care facility. In this section, I share some of my insight into and experiences with dementia care.

It was opening day for a new, state-of-the-art care facility for veterans. One year had passed since I had accepted an offer to join an architectural team as the dementia consultant. The company had been awarded a contract by the Florida Department of Veterans' Affairs to build several nursing facilities throughout the state for the care of military veterans. Each facility would contain a dementia unit.

During my social work career, I spent more than 20 years working with persons with memory loss and their caregivers. It was my personal experience with my own family members that led me to focus on dementia care in much of my practice, teaching, and research. I had watched my grandmother and later my mother develop and struggle with dementia. In the 1960s, when my grandfather could no longer take care of my grandmother, she was refused admission to nursing homes because they were unable to deal with her behaviors. With no other options, she spent her last 2 years in a psychiatric hospital. Twenty-five years later, there were still no dementia care residences when my mother had to be placed in a nursing home. For the rest of my family, my mother's death signified the end of their journey as caregivers. In my own experience as a social worker and educator, I continued to assist others who were caring for persons with dementia.

It had taken the architectural team a year to plan and build the new cutting-edge residence for veterans. My role as dementia consultant was to plan a section of the building for residents who had significant short-term memory loss, but whose remaining long-term memories were of serving in the military during World War II or the Korean War. The living environment was designed to foster those memories— common areas had murals lining the walls depicting scenes of Parisian cafes and the streets and landscapes of Europe, including a barber- shop, stores, and an ice cream parlor all located along "Main Street." The cafeteria was labeled "Mess Hall," and the bathroom signs read, "Latrine." There was a flagpole in the enclosed courtyard designed for daily flag-raising and flag-lowering ceremonies, and the front of a truck was attached to one of the walls, with engine intact for the "mechanics" on the unit.

As the first resident left the admissions office and started down the hallway toward the dementia unit, his wife cautioned him, "You know, the person who will be in charge of this unit is a woman."

"Oh, I don't think I am going to like taking orders from a woman," he said.

"But," his wife replied, "she is a general."

"I guess that is okay," the resident replied as the door to the unit opened. He saluted the head nurse, who wore a 1940s Army nurse uniform decorated with bars and stripes.

Dementia care units promise to provide better care for individuals with dementia than what is available in the traditional long-term care setting. The premise that a therapeutic model will improve functioning and qual- ity of life for persons with dementia appears to be valid.[7] The following are special features of a dementia care program:

- *Therapeutic activities*: Residents are grouped homogeneously for activities and other functions based on their physical and mental functioning. Goals include re-motivation, sensory stimulation, reminiscence, and validation therapy. These activities are provided 7 days a week in appropriate settings.

- *Restorative treatment plans:* A restorative physical and occupational therapy treatment plan is established for each resident to maximize his or her potential in performing activities of daily living and preventing, as much as possible, further deterioration.

- *Medical care:* Medical diagnostic and therapeutic techniques are utilized by physicians and other members of the healthcare team who have specific training and interest in dementia. Collaborative relationships are established with community medical professionals and facilities.

- *Family support:* Counseling is provided to help families understand the disease process and the feelings that they may experience during their family member's illness. Families are also educated about the philosophy and goals of the dementia program and are involved in care planning. Family support groups with professional leadership are established to provide information on dementia, assist families in planning for the care of their relatives and issues affecting their care (e.g., financial, legal, medical, and social), and assist families in coping with the emotional factors involved when a relative has dementia.

Healthcare professionals working with older adults who have dementia need thorough training on how to provide these critical elements of dementia care. They also need support with professional roles that, though rewarding, could also be difficult and emotional work. Using the following exercise, I helped dementia care staff come to terms with some of the emotional challenges of their caregiving responsibilities:

At the beginning of class, blank sheets of paper were handed out, and staff were asked to draw a line down the center of the paper. On one side, they were told to write down aspects of their work with residents that gave them satisfaction. On the opposite side, they were to write down the negative elements of their job that caused them to feel stressed. Participants were then asked to share their comments with the group.

Many of the staff expressed frustration that, while attention was focused on helping residents cope with the death of their friends and roommates, little or no attention was paid to the feelings of loss and grief felt by the staff who had cared for them for months and sometimes years. Instead, they were expected to come to work the next day and care for the new resident who was now occupying the deceased person's room.

With the help of the facility's administrator, I established a policy that allowed staff the opportunity to grieve for the loss of their residents. When a death occurred, the resident's family was encouraged to communicate directly with the caregiver. Many times, the family would give the caregiver a small item that had belonged to the resident. Once a month, the facility held a memorial for residents who had passed away that month. Families were invited, as well as the residents' caregivers, who were asked to share their memories and stories. The caregivers' remarks provided comfort and closure for the families in knowing that their loved one had caregivers who cared.

This example illustrates how input from long-term care staff can translate into important policy changes. Staff training in dementia care is now mandated in several states. Training staff in strategies and interventions that promote dignity and quality of life for individuals with dementia benefits residents and reduces stress for staff.

CHAPTER NOTES

1. The Administration for Community Living (ACL). (2018). *2018 profile of older Americans.* Washington, DC: Author. Retrieved from https://acl.gov/sites/default/files/Aging%20and%20Disability%20in%20America/2018OlderAmericansProfile.pdf

2. Harris-Kojetin, L., Sengupta, M., Park-Lee, E., Valverde, R., Caffrey, C., Rome, V., et al. (2016). *Long-term care providers and services users in the United States: Data from the National Study of Long-Term Care Providers, 2013–2014* (Vital & Health Statistics, Series 3, No. 38). Hyattsville, MD: U.S. Department of Health and Human Services, Centers for Disease Control and Prevention, National Center for Health Statistics. Retrieved from https://www.cdc.gov/nchs/data/series/sr_03/sr03_038.pdf

3. The National Association of Social Workers (NASW). (2003). *NASW Standards for Social Work Services in Long-Term Care Facilities.* Washington, DC: NASW.

4. Beaulieu, E.M. (2002). *A guide for nursing home social workers.* New York: Springer Publishing Company.

5. Bach, P.L., & Meyers, P.G. (2013). *Sexuality in long-term care.* Columbia, MD: The Society for Post-Acute and Long-Term Care Medicine (AMDA).

6. For further reading about sexuality in nursing home settings, see Doll, G. (2012). *Sexuality and long-term care: Understanding and supporting the needs of older adults.* Baltimore: Health Professions Press; Doll, G. (2013). Sexuality in nursing homes: Practice and policy. *Journal of Gerontological Nursing, 39*(7), 30–37; Lichtenberg, P.A. (2014). Sexuality and physical intimacy in long-term care. *Occupational Therapy in Health Care, 28*(1), 42–50; Levine, M. (2016). Sex and the nursing home. *American Journal of Orthopsychiatry, 86*(3), 355–359; Hu, W. (2016, July 12). Too old for sex? Not at this nursing home. *The New York Times.* Retrieved from https://www.nytimes.com/2016/07/13/nyregion/too-old-for-sex-not-at-this-nursing-home.html

7. Hoffman, S.B., & Kaplan, M. (1996). *Special care programs for people with dementia.* Baltimore: Health Professions Press.

CHAPTER 14

Geriatric Care Management

KEY POINTS

- Geriatric care managers coordinate the service delivery system, facilitating family support and providing counseling and direct services when necessary to ensure a comprehensive care plan.

- The growth of private geriatric care managers has emerged in response to the increasing complexity and fragmentation of services for older adults and the inability of families to provide continuing care.

- Social work education and training prepare social workers to perform the core functions of care management.

WHEN OLDER ADULTS NEED HELP, they usually receive it from families or a combination of family care and an assortment of community-based health and social services. The systems of care that serve older adults are not well coordinated. This not only makes it difficult for older clients to access needed services, but it also means that social workers often do not have adequate knowledge about the wide range of services available to older adults. Geriatric care managers serve as "navigators" and "expediters," enabling older adults and their families to understand and choose from the array of available health and social services. When necessary, they facilitate family support, provide counseling and direct services, and coordinate care. Care management is used to coordinate different segments of the service delivery system to ensure a comprehensive plan that meets an individual's needs.

Although often thought of as a relatively new concept, care management has long been a part of traditional social work practice. Care management programs that focus on older adults arose out of the community action programs of the 1950s and 1960s and legislation in the 1970s. The Allied Services Act, proposed in 1971, improved coordination among programs of the Department of Health, Education, and Welfare (now the Department of Health and Human Services), and the 1978 Amendment to the Older Americans Act implemented case management through Area Agencies on Aging. Other federal and state programs that initiated a care management approach in their services for older adults included Triage in Connecticut, On Lok in San Francisco, and ACCESS in New York.

Over the past 40 years, private geriatric care management has emerged in response to the increasing complexity and fragmentation of services for older adults and the inability of families to provide continuing care to their older members. Increased mobility and changes in family structure and roles have made it difficult for families to assume caregiving responsibilities. For example, smaller families mean fewer children to share the caregiving role for an aging parent, the increase of women in the workplace has left fewer women in the home to provide care, and the increase in divorce and the rise of the single-parent family have limited family resources, both emotional and economic. In addition, the demographic trend of increased longevity means that some elders are caring for older parents.

In 1983, the New England Long-Term Care Center at Brown University in Providence, Rhode Island identified 22 private geriatric care managers.[1] Located primarily in the Northeast, these care managers linked clients and community-based support services, helped clients process health insurance forms, and counseled families. In 1985, the National Association of Private Geriatric Care Managers (NAPGCM) was organized when the Greater New York Network for Aging, a local, private geriatric care management organization, sponsored the first national conference on private geriatric care management.[1] During the next 2 years, guidelines for standards, membership, and organizational structure were formulated, and a board of directors was elected, which established committees and developed the association's bylaws. Membership consisted of approximately 50 members (mostly social workers and nurses) who were business owners and who had a minimum of a master's degree and 2 years of supervised experience in a geriatric care setting.

The NAPGCM was a trade association—one dedicated to increasing members and positioning those members to develop businesses in the newly emerging field. Over the years, the association worked to elevate professional standards and criteria for membership, eventually changing its name to the National Association of Professional Geriatric Care Managers (NAPGCM). In 1995, the National Academy of Certified Care Managers was established to offer certification for care managers. Care managers who meet the education, experience, and supervision requirements must pass a standardized examination to become certified. Certification is renewed every 3 years, and care managers are required to participate in continuing education and professional development.[2]

Comprehensive services provided by care managers include assessment (functional, social, and financial), evaluation and placement of clients in alternative living arrangements, referral and coordination of community services, and ongoing monitoring of client and support services. In addition to care management, direct services are also offered, such as counseling for clients and caregivers. The following story describes my work with a client who was referred to me by a national referral network for care management services.[3]

The initial request for services came from the client's daughter, who lived in another state and was concerned about her father's ability to care for her mother, Alice. Alice was exhibiting some memory loss and personality changes as a result of a stroke. Her daughter had made several trips to set up home care, which Alice promptly terminated.

Assessment:

A former chemical engineer retired for 15 years, Ben was an articulate, well-groomed man who looked younger than his 85 years. He stated that since his wife, Alice, had a stroke several months ago, he had been responsible for her care in addition to doing the cooking, shopping, and gardening. Progressive arthritis in both knees and general fatigue caused by his strenuous routine had made him feel somewhat overwhelmed by his caregiving responsibilities. Frustrated by his wife's dependency, Ben expressed resentment at no longer being able to get out socially and enjoy his hobbies. Yet, he was very proud of the care he had given his wife, and he planned to continue caring for her as long as he was able.

Alice was a 79-year-old retired school teacher who was recovering from a stroke. She exhibited left-sided weakness and used a walker to ambulate. She was oriented to time and place but had some short-term memory loss. She also had difficulty remembering names, relying on her husband to fill in the gaps. She had no memory of her hospitalization or nursing home stay, which had occurred 6 months earlier. In addition to the lingering effects of the stroke, Alice also had a chronic lung condition that caused congestion and coughing. She admitted relying extensively on her husband for assistance. When questioned as to why she had terminated home care services, she insisted that the quality of the services was poor.

Ben and Alice had two daughters who lived in other states and no family that lived nearby. They did have several friends who visited occasionally, but Alice had only recently started accompanying her husband on outings. The couple lived in a well-kept, three-bedroom, one-story house. Ben was currently doing all the housework and maintaining the yard. Alice insisted that she helped with the housework and cooking, although her husband stated that she could not perform anything but the simplest of tasks.

Care Plan:

1. Occupational therapy consultation for Alice to (a) assess personal care skills and further rehabilitation potential; (b) recommend adaptive equipment to allow her to function more independently; (c) evaluate contracture of her left hand, splinting if necessary; and (d) educate her on the use of energy-saving techniques for personal care and light housework

2. Neurological consultation to evaluate Alice's cognitive impairment

3. Counseling and support for Ben to enable him to cope with the reality of his wife's condition and to allow him to express his anger and frustration about his caregiving responsibilities

4. Homemaker aide services to aid with housework and provide a companion sitter for Alice to give Ben some respite from caregiving

5. Weekly home visits by the care manager for counseling and monitoring of support services

6. Encouragement for the couple to use community support services

Community Service Linkage:

As care manager, I contacted a home health agency and arranged for an occupational therapist to come to the home to evaluate Alice's physical disabilities and to suggest adaptive equipment and energy-saving techniques to improve her personal care skills. The agency also scheduled a homemaker aide twice a week to help with the housework and to stay with Alice to give Ben some free time. A referral was made to a memory loss clinic to assess Alice's dementia symptoms.

When Alice was hospitalized for a hip fracture as a result of a fall, I planned for short-term nursing home placement and then set up home care services, which included a weekly visit by a nurse, daily visits by a home health aide, and physical therapy sessions. Ben was encouraged to attend family support meetings offered by the local stroke club each month. Arrangements were made for the home health aide to stay with Alice when Ben went to the meetings and when he went shopping.

Monitoring:

Weekly visits to the couple by the care manager continued for a year. During this time, changes in both Ben's and Alice's conditions were noted, and the care plan was revised. In addition, the consistency and quality of the care being provided were monitored. On several occasions, I found that home health aides were not showing up as scheduled. This finding resulted in the agency's services being terminated and a referral being made to another agency. As the care manager, I was able to cross the boundaries between different levels of care and help address limitations of service imposed by health care facilities and community agencies. In several instances, I followed Ben and Alice through hospitalization, nursing home care, and home care.

When Alice's mental and physical condition became too difficult for Ben to handle at home, he made the decision to move to a more supportive environment. As care manager, I researched the local housing options and took Ben to look at several retirement communities that provided nursing home care as well as independent living arrangements. Ben chose a church-sponsored retirement community that would allow him to live in a small cottage within walking distance of the nursing care center where Alice would be placed. I assisted with the application process as well as the move. Following the move, I continued to visit the couple biweekly.

Two years later, while on a trip to visit his daughter, Ben had a stroke. Although his recovery went well, there was general agreement among Ben, his family, and me that it was time for Ben and Alice to move closer to their family. After 3 years, care management services were terminated when the couple moved into a retirement community near one of their daughters.

Advocacy:

On several occasions when Ben expressed concern and frustration over not being able to obtain proper medical treatment, I intervened as the care manager. Often, the intervention resulted in a change in medication or physician. In one situation, both Ben and I became concerned about the number of medications being administered to Alice in the nursing home, which caused her to become lethargic and more confused. With my support and assurance that it was okay for Ben to be assertive about his wife's care, Ben requested a review of Alice's medications and was able to get them reduced.

Caregiver Support:

Initial counseling with Ben was directed toward providing support and allowing him to express his feelings about his caregiving responsibilities. Supportive counseling continued to be provided to Ben to help him deal with the guilt that he experienced when Alice fell and had to be placed in a nursing home.

Separate visits were often scheduled with Ben to discuss the stress he experienced in his caregiving role and to assess his own needs and capabilities. As care manager, I encouraged him to take some time for himself and to leave the house when the home health aide arrived.

When Alice became more confused and combative and was unable to function without total assistance, sessions with Ben became focused on making a decision about long-term care placement. In addition to helping Ben locate a long-term care setting for Alice, I assisted him in finding a supportive living environment for himself. Counseling prior to, during, and following the move helped to ease the trauma of relocation for Ben. Counseling also helped him adjust to changes in his caregiving role. For example, when Ben's visits to the nursing center several times a day caused Alice to become agitated and resistive to care, he was persuaded to set up a schedule that limited his visits to once a day.

The rapid growth in the specialty of geriatric care management has created many opportunities for social workers. Social work education and training in geriatrics prepare social workers for the core functions of care management, which include comprehensive assessment; care plan development and implementation; monitoring and evaluation; and knowledge of long-term care issues, such as aging and disability issues, community services, benefit and financing options, and legal and ethical concerns.

In addition to the growth of private geriatric care management, the use of care managers has become common in publicly funded state and local home- and community-based care programs across the country. These programs employ or contract for social workers to assess a person's need for long-term care services and to organize the delivery of services. Many geriatric care managers began their careers in these publicly funded programs and may move on to private geriatric care practice.

CHAPTER NOTES

1. Fauri, D.P., & Bradford, J.B. (1986). Practice with the frail elderly in the private sector. *Families in Society: The Journal of Contemporary Social Services*, 67(5), 259–265.

2. Kaplan, M. (1988). Private geriatric case management. In K. Fisher & E. Weisman (Eds.), *Case management: Guiding patients through the health care maze* (pp. 57–58). Oakbrook Terrace, IL: The Joint Commission on Accreditation of Healthcare Organizations.

3. National Academy of Certified Care Managers Home Page. Retrieved September 18, 2019 at https://www.naccm.net/about/purpose-goals/

4. Kaplan, M. (1996). *Clinical practice with caregivers of dementia patients*. Washington, DC: Taylor & Francis.

Community Agencies and Services

- Social workers are trained and qualified to assist older adults and their families to make informed decisions about care and to access the appropriate resources to meet their needs.

- Many domestic violence programs fail to recognize and serve older victims of abuse.

- Community agencies that serve older adults face challenges in addressing the racial, cultural, ethnic, religious, and gender diversity of clients.

SOCIAL WORKERS PROVIDE an important link between older adults and the services that they need. Regardless of the setting in which a social worker practices, it is important to understand the network of aging services well enough to assist when necessary. Therapy with older adults often focuses on the complexity of their problems and the need for intervention in psychosocial areas of their lives. Because medical and social problems may be prominent for older clients, there is often the need to work within a biopsychosocial model. The term "casework services" can refer to two types of activities: (1) providing accurate information on available services for problems the client has that fall outside the scope of therapy and (2) providing or setting up services for the client.

Available Agencies and Services for Older Adults

Service systems for older adults are often complex and have various rules about eligibility. Each community has a different network of services, but these programs are generally available in most communities that provide services to older adults:

- Area Agencies on Aging (https://eldercare.acl.gov)

- County eldercare services

- Family service agencies

- Disease-specific associations (e.g., Alzheimer's Association, Arthritis Association)

- Community mental health associations

- Congregate meal sites and home-delivered meal programs

- Senior recreation centers

- Adult day care

- Income-assistance programs

- Transportation services

- Hospital-based programs

- Legal services

- Emergency services that provide food or pay utility bills

Without information about community resources and counseling from qualified professionals, older adults and their families are often unable to make informed decisions about care and to access the appropriate resources to meet their needs. Social workers are uniquely trained and qualified to provide these services. Below, I provide an example of a situation in which a community service program was inadequate in addressing the specific needs of older adults.

One of my community volunteer experiences was at a county domestic violence shelter, where I covered for the staff on weekends and was a member of the board of directors, serving a term as board president.

This program provided emergency services for women and their children who had experienced domestic violence, offering shelter and counseling. Community education was also an important service offered by the program, helping people to recognize domestic violence, to understand its effects on the victim and family, and to work to break the cycle of violence. One weekend each month, I carried a pager and was responsible for taking calls from the sheriff's department and admitting domestic violence victims to the shelter. My volunteer hours began late Friday afternoon and ended Monday morning when the shelter staff arrived. It was not unusual to receive my first call as I was leaving my job at the hospital on a Friday evening. I would arrive at the sheriff's office, or in some cases, at the hospital emergency room where the victim had been treated, and transport her to the shelter.

The location of the shelter was kept secret to protect its residents. The dilapidated two-story house sat between a vacant lot and an empty building on the edge of downtown. The program staff consisted of a director and several women who were trained as peer counselors. The women who came to the shelter often lacked self-esteem, were emotionally and financially dependent, and had difficulty making decisions. Counseling was directed toward helping clients identify needs and set goals. Group counseling was also offered to shelter residents, as well as to women still in a battering relationship and those shelter "alumni" who had reestablished their lives in the community. Referrals for professional counseling were made to a clinical psychologist in the community.

One of the drawbacks to the program was that the shelter was for women only. The few male victims of domestic violence were housed at a motel. The program also failed to serve another group: older adults. The shelter was not accessible for frail elders or individuals with disabilities, and it was not wheelchair accessible. To reach the bedrooms, the shelter residents had to climb a steep flight of stairs, and the bathrooms were small and lacked any adaptive modifications. Counseling and education were not directed toward older victims of domestic violence.

In my experience as a shelter volunteer, I encountered only one elder victim—an 80-year-old man who had been battered by his wife. At that time, it was unusual to receive referrals for elder victims of domestic abuse. The extent of abuse against older adults had been a well-kept secret and was only beginning to be discovered and acknowledged by society at the time.

Cases in which the abuse of an older person is perpetrated by a spouse or intimate partner tend to go unrecognized. For many years, the lack of social response to elder abuse was fueled by the ageist perception that all intimate partner and family relationships between older adults were harmonious, respectful, and supportive. It was also perceived that the older victim of abuse had fewer options for leaving an abusive situation.[1,2]

Many community agencies have developed specific programs and services to meet the special needs of the growing older population. These services should have the following features:

- Services should be designed to fit older people rather than forcing older people to fit into categorical services.

- Services should be developed around the life roles and challenges of older adults.

Agencies that serve older adults face challenges in addressing the cultural, racial, ethnic, and religious diversity of their clients. Social isolation, inadequate community outreach, and limited English proficiency and language barriers play a large role in keeping minority elders from accessing services. Differing views about health and medical treatment; resistance to applying for services and asking for help; and the reluctance of older adults from some cultures to take directions from younger professionals of a different ethnicity, gender, or culture can serve as additional barriers to services.

The following guidelines for practice and policy should help to improve sensitivity to the needs of minority elders:

- As much as possible, staff members should represent the diversity of the clients they serve, especially in the provision of outreach, case management, and counseling services.

- Funding and contracting procedures should be reviewed to ensure that minority aging organizations are given the opportunity to be providers of aging services.

- Agencies should use culturally appropriate sites, people, and materials for outreach to their client populations. For example, outreach programs to the African American community should include churches and traditional African American sororities and fraternal organizations; materials for the Hispanic community should be printed in Spanish; and outreach efforts to Native Americans should involve tribal councils and other Native American health and social services organizations.

- The demographics of the community should be regularly reviewed to determine the composition of the older population and the subgroups that may be present within each ethnic group. For example, the Asian population may include Vietnamese and Cambodian immigrants whose culture is significantly different from Chinese or Japanese Americans. Older adults who are identified as Hispanic or Latino are also members of diverse subgroups that originated from Mexico, Puerto Rico, South America, and Central America.

- If language is a barrier, an interpreter may be necessary and can also help with service resistance by framing the discussion of receiving services in a culturally acceptable way. When obtaining information, questions can be asked in several ways to ensure that older clients and their families understand and provide a relevant response. Saying "no" in some cultures is viewed as impolite.

Many social workers work in community settings that provide services and care for older adults. Social workers help aging individuals and their families navigate the often-confusing systems of community care. They provide counseling on programs and services available in the community and act as advocates, offering advice and assistance with applying for services. This often involves helping to clarify the wishes of the older adult when he or she is unable to understand or communicate because of disability or language barriers.

Social work administrators can be proactive leaders in public and private agencies that provide services to older clients. Many elements of social work practice are common to administration in other organizations. However, administration and management of community agencies for older adults also require knowledge about social policy and the delivery of social services, a vision for future planning, an understanding of diversity and human behavior, and a commitment to social work ethics and values.

CHAPTER NOTES

1. Jacobs, R., Kane, M., & Green, D. (2011). Perceptions of intimate partner violence, age, and self-enhancement bias. *Journal of Elder Abuse & Neglect, 23*(1), 89–114. doi:10.1080/08946566.2011.534710.

2.   For further reading about domestic violence and older adults, see Crockett, C.,
      Brandl, B., & Dabby, F.C. (2015). Survivors in the margins: The invisibility of
      violence against older women. *Journal of Elder Abuse & Neglect, 27*(4-5), 291-302;
      Brandl, B., Hebert, M., Spangler, D., & Rozwadowski, J. (2003). Feeling safe, feel-
      ing strong: Support groups for older abused women. *Violence Against Women, 9*(12),
      1490-1503; Danis, F.S. (2003). Social work response to domestic violence: Encour-
      aging news from a new look. *Affilia: Journal of Women and Social Work, 18*(2) 177-191;
      National Association of Social Workers (NASW). (2018). Family violence policy
      statement. In *Social work speaks: National Association of Social Workers Policy State-
      ments 2018-2020* (11th ed.) (pp 127-133). Washington, DC: NASW Press.

CHAPTER 16

Psychiatric Settings

KEY POINTS

- The community mental health model of care was developed in the 1960s and 1970s to care for patients who had been discharged to the community following the closing of many psychiatric hospitals.

- Psychiatric social workers in outpatient settings provide therapy and care coordination services to persons who have mental illnesses and debilitative emotional and/or behavioral issues.

- Inpatient psychiatric social workers work primarily in psychiatric departments of hospitals and medical centers with patients who have been hospitalized for debilitating or dangerous psychiatric and/or behavioral issues.

THE COMMUNITY MENTAL HEALTH ACT of 1963 (PL 88-164), signed by President John F. Kennedy, was designed to provide federal funding for the construction of community-based preventative care and treatment facilities for mental health. This legislation was part of a movement to deinstitutionalize individuals with mental illnesses that had begun during the 1950s, with the plan to transfer homeless, involuntarily hospitalized psychiatric patients from state mental hospitals into supervised community housing funded by the federal government. Mental health reform and the increased scrutiny of institutions helped to expose poor conditions and treatment and revealed that these institutions created dependency and disability in the patients. It was thought that community services would be less expensive and that new psychiatric medications would facilitate the release of people into the community. This resulted in the closing of many inpatient psychiatric treatment facilities.[1]

As a social worker who seriously considered a career in mental health, I have witnessed the continued need for compassionate, quality mental health services for older adults firsthand. In the following story, I share an example of the historical mistreatment and inadequate care of individuals with mental health conditions.

Project Launchpad was a program developed in Buffalo in 1971 to provide transitional housing and services for deinstitutionalized clients living with serious mental illnesses. The clients were released into the community when the Buffalo Psychiatric Hospital closed several of its wards as part of the country's movement away from inpatient treatment to direct funding toward community mental healthcare. I was a B.S.W student at the University of Buffalo and was considering working in the mental health field after graduation, so I decided to volunteer at the project's halfway house.

My role was to help and support several residents at the house as they learned to function in the community after many years as inpatients in a psychiatric hospital. Simple everyday activities, such as shopping, taking public transportation, and using the laundromat, presented a challenge as they tried to adjust to community life. It soon became evident that there were serious obstacles to the success of this particular program.

One factor contributing to the program's lack of success was that the halfway house was in a neighborhood that was known for its high rates of poverty and crime. The residents, some elders, were a vulnerable group struggling with serious mental health disabilities and deficient social skills, so they became easy targets of crime. Another contributing factor to the program's failure was the inability of the community mental health model to provide needed services for this high-risk population. Following their discharge from the hospital, program participants were assigned case managers and were told to report to the community mental health center, where they would receive their medications. We soon discovered that some clients were not taking their medications but were selling them on the street. I became increasingly concerned about the clients, who were experiencing delusions and engaging in violent behaviors. Several were found to be incapable of living in the community and returned to the hospital. The following excerpt from my journal describes my encounters with Project Launchpad's residents:

As I made my way up the steps leading to the front porch of the dilapidated house, I was met by several of the residents, who wanted to know if I had any cigarettes. Upon learning that I had nothing to offer, they returned to the chairs that were lined up along the porch railing. My knock on the front door was answered by the resident manager, who brought me into the living room. The room was sparsely furnished with a few chairs and a well-worn flowered sofa, where two of the residents sat dozing.

In the dining room, I found the man who was to be my client. John was sitting at the dining room table with another man, both with a cigarette in hand. I noticed that there was very little conversation or interaction between any of the residents, and I soon understood the reason. My weekly visits with John were usually spent sitting on the flowered sofa or at the dining room table. Although the goal of the program was to teach the residents how to navigate life and function in the community, it became evident that their psychiatric disorders and often barbaric treatment in the psychiatric hospital, along with many years of hospitalization, made this goal unrealistic without the appropriate supports and services in place.

Conversations with John and the other residents were difficult because several clients had undergone lobotomies, and all were on heavy psychiatric medications that impaired functioning and judgment. In fact, the only time that I saw any animation or expression in these individuals was when they were engaged in a confrontation with the resident manager or other residents. John's conversations were often not based in reality. During one of my visits, he showed me a copy of Playboy *magazine and, turning to the centerfold, announced that the woman on the page was in fact his girlfriend and that they were dating.*

One day I arrived to find that John was no longer there. He had gotten into a violent altercation with another resident and was readmitted to the psychiatric hospital.

This experience illustrated for me the desperate need for better mental health treatment. The failure of the community to provide care and services to members of this vulnerable population and my inability to improve their lives left me with feelings of sadness and a sense of frustration.

––––––––––––––––––

When Medicare was first implemented in 1965, it paid only for inpatient psychiatric treatment. It wasn't until the late 1980s that coverage was extended to mental health services in outpatient settings, which led to the expansion of geriatric mental health programs. Psychiatric social workers in outpatient settings provide therapy and care coordination services to individuals who do not require hospitalization, but who still struggle with severe mental illness and debilitating emotional and/or behavioral issues. These individuals are often at risk of needing hospitalization or have recently been discharged from an inpatient setting. Outpatient psychiatric social workers tend to work for an extended period of time with geriatric clients and may even follow them through multiple systems to help support them as they transition from hospitalization to home or to another facility.

One of the most important responsibilities of the psychiatric social worker is to conduct diagnostic assessments of mental health in order to determine a person's specific psychological issues and needs. The following scenario from my career illustrates how social workers can use information gained from risk assessments to evaluate whether an individual is mentally competent to make life decisions and/or if that person may experience adverse outcomes in his or her current state and situation.

From 1995 to 2004, I served on an examining committee for guardianship under the 13th Judicial Circuit Court in Florida. I received a request from the Office of the Public Defender to evaluate the mental capacity of an older woman, Ms. Knight, who had been charged as a public nuisance by the city. The order provided the following information:

Client appears to have a possible mental health disability. She stated that the city was "out to get her" because she is feeding animals on her property. She said that it is "God's rule" that anything that comes on her property should be fed. Client also claims to be suffering from several medical problems, stating that she needs open-heart surgery and has a brain tumor. The client indicated that she has had problems with the city in the past when they came and took 48 dogs from her yard. Recently, she has been feeding cats on her property. She puts out a table of food for them. She stated that part of her yard belongs to God and that "a person wouldn't want to have starving cats around because they could attack a puppy." She said that she lives in one room of her house and can't sleep in her bed, so she sleeps on the floor. She also stated that she only eats once a day because that is when Meals on Wheels comes to her house. She is supposed to have her yard cleaned up by her next court date. Could we have someone go to her house and check on her and the progress of her clean-up? She may need to be Baker Acted [institutionalized under the Florida law that allows the involuntary institutionalization and evaluation of an individual when he or she is at risk of harm to self or others].

In response, a client evaluation and home evaluation were completed, and the report shown in Table 16.1 was filed with the court.

Table 16.1 Mental Capacity And Sanity Evaluation: Ms. Knight

The Defendant, *Ms. Knight*, was referred to the Examiner, *Mary Kaplan, LCSW* for the purpose of determining the Defendant's capacity to:	
A	Appreciate the charges or allegations against her;
B	Appreciate the range and nature of possible penalties, which may be imposed in the proceedings;
C	Understand the adversary nature of the legal process;
D	Disclose to defense attorney facts pertinent to the proceedings at issue; manifest appropriate courtroom behavior; and
E	Testify relevantly.

Table 16.1 *Continued*

	Evaluation Methods: The methods used to examine and evaluate the Defendant consisted of the following:
A	The Mini-Mental State Examination (MMSE), a screening tool that evaluates cognitive functioning (short-term memory, orientation to time and place, eye-hand coordination, ability to follow instruction, and ability to calculate numbers);
B	Hazard recognition, in which the Defendant was presented with a hazardous scenario and asked to explain her response to the situation;
C	Interview, to obtain information about the Defendant's history, medical status, family, finances, her perceptions of her needs and her ability to meet those needs, and her understanding of the charges against her;
D	Observation of the Defendant during the interview, to include physical appearance, quality of communication, and behavior; and
E	Observation of the Defendant's physical environment, to evaluate safety and health hazards.

Clinical Observations and Findings

Ms. Knight is a 77-year-old white female who appears to be well nourished and in no apparent distress. She showed signs of self-neglect, specifically poor hygiene. She wore no shoes, and her feet and nails were dirty. There was a noticeable body odor of urine. Her clothing, a flowered, loose-fitting dress, was appropriate and clean.

Ms. Knight ambulates without assistance, although she stated that she uses a wheelchair because she tires easily. There was an electric wheelchair with various items stacked on it located inside the house by the front door. When asked to show me around her property, Ms. Knight walked from the front yard to the backyard, slowly and unsteadily. She exhibited some difficulty breathing after walking a short distance and had to sit down to rest several times. She required some assistance in returning to her front yard. Her manual dexterity appears to be normal. She was able to hold a pencil without difficulty and to write a sentence and copy a design legibly.

Ms. Knight displays no impairment in language, either receptively or expressively. She was exceedingly talkative and attempted to dominate the conversation.

Behavior

Ms. Knight was cooperative although reluctant to allow the interviewer to enter her house. She responded to questions without hesitation, often expressing anger at the court for removing her [48] dogs from her home and at her sons for taking some of her possessions.

Mental Status

Ms. Knight does not show signs of cognitive impairment and had a score of 30 out of a total of 30 points on the MMSE. She is oriented to person, place, and time; can complete serial computations; and does not exhibit short-term memory loss. Although she acknowledges that her health is poor, she denies that there is any reason for her to make changes in her environment or that she needs additional assistance.

Table 16.1   *Continued*

Environment

Ms. Knight was sitting in her driveway when I arrived and explained that she lives outside most of the time. There were a van and a car in the driveway, both in poor condition and filled with some of Ms. Knight's possessions. When questioned as to her use of the vehicles, she responded that she is no longer driving because of her increased vision loss. She was willing to show me her backyard but stated that she did not want me to go inside the house. Inspection of the backyard revealed massive piles of household articles, lawn equipment (including five lawnmowers), appliances, medical equipment, clothing, and garbage. Some of the articles were contained in large plastic storage boxes. When she opened the boxes to show me the contents, roaches crawled out.
 	
    When asked about toilet facilities, she opened a door in the back of the house to reveal a small room consisting of a toilet and a handheld shower device. There was no sink in the bathroom and no access from inside the house—she must go out the front door and walk around to the backyard to use the bathroom. There was a washing machine in the backyard that was plugged into an outside outlet. She stated that she uses it to wash her clothes. Piles of assorted articles were visible in the windows at the back of the house.
 	
    Despite Ms. Knight's objections, I was able to enter the room at the front of the house through the front door. It did not appear that she had access to other rooms—they were blocked off by piles of clothing and household items. When asked about food storage and meal preparation, she replied that she stores food in the refrigerator and cooks in the microwave. Upon inspection, I saw that both the microwave and the refrigerator doors were blocked and were not easily accessible. There was a carton of eggs sitting on top of the microwave and bags of candy located throughout the room. There was a mattress in the middle of the room and a TV on top of the stove. The TV was turned on. Electrical cords were running across the entry throughout the room, and a space heater, which was turned on, was located by the front door. There was also a phone next to the front door. Ms. Knight stated that she and her neighbors had been having problems with their electricity switching off and on and that she had complained to the electric company. When asked what she would do if a fire broke out in the house, she replied that she would get up off the mattress and go out the front door.

History: *The information regarding Ms. Knight's medical and family history was provided by the Defendant and may not be completely reliable:*

1. Medical	Ms. Knight's history of heart disease, including cardiac bypass surgery, has been substantiated by the social worker for the Public Defender's Office. Following her surgery, Ms. Knight was in a nursing home for a month. She stated that she has been diagnosed with a brain tumor that is affecting her vision and is scheduled for surgery, but she was unable to give me the date of the anticipated procedure. She also stated that she takes medication for heart disease, which she gets at the nearby military base when she can get someone to drive her there.
2. Family	Ms. Knight stated that her husband of 61 years died one year ago following an extended illness. She said that she has three children, two sons and a daughter, as well as several grandchildren. She told me that all her children were "perfect." She did not indicate that she has frequent contact with her children except for her occasional references to her son, who she says came to her house when she was in the hospital and threw away some of her possessions. According to the court social worker, Ms. Knight also has a brother and sister-in-law who have made attempts to assist her, but Ms. Knight would not listen to them.

Table 16.1 *Continued*

Summary and Recommendations
It is clear that Ms. Knight's current living conditions are unsafe and present an immediate threat to her health and safety. Her heart disease, the possibility of a brain tumor, and possible vision loss make it physically impossible for her to make the necessary changes to her property that the court requires. Although she has made some attempts to hire people to clear her yard, she is incapable of following through with completion of this task and has difficulty letting go of her possessions regardless of their value and condition. She is also vulnerable to potential exploitation and harm by others. Although she does not appear to exhibit signs of dementia, neurological impairment caused by her brain tumor cannot be ruled out at this time. Her hoarding behavior and her rationalization for her behavior are suggestive of an obsessive-compulsive disorder. If this is the case, then she lacks the ability to reason accurately and to make good decisions. It is my recommendation that any legal charges against Ms. Knight be suspended until further medical assessment and treatment have been completed. In the meantime, steps should be taken to appoint a guardian to assist Ms. Knight in obtaining necessary medical care and addressing her unsafe living environment.

Inpatient psychiatric social workers work primarily in psychiatry departments of hospitals and medical centers with patients who have been hospitalized for debilitating or dangerous psychological and/or behavioral issues. They conduct psychosocial assessments to determine patients' mental health status and needs; help patients address their emotional, behavioral, and mental health challenges; communicate and coordinate with the treatment team to optimize patients' physical and mental health care; connect patients with resources and services; and facilitate patients' transition to other care facilities or back home through discharge planning. Depending on their work setting, psychiatric social workers may deliver short-term or long-term psychotherapy to patients, utilizing different clinical social work methods according to each patient's situation and needs. My past experiences working in a psychiatric hospital provide a glimpse into some issues commonly faced by older adults in inpatient psychiatric settings.

During the mid-1990s, I worked for a brief time at an inpatient psychiatric hospital that was located on the University of South Florida campus. As the social worker for the Senior Adult Unit, I was a member of the unit's multidisciplinary team, making recommendations for treatment and discharge plans. It was a small unit with an average patient census of 10 to 15 patients. Approximately half of our geriatric patients had admitting diagnoses of serious mental illnesses, with the remaining number admitted for behavioral problems related to cognitive impairment. Often, an individual would be admitted from a long-term care setting for behavior that was disruptive to staff or other residents and would be extremely agitated and confused. These patients, upon evaluation, were often found to be suffering from adverse reactions to medication, overmedication, or undiagnosed urinary tract infections (UTIs). Once their medication was eliminated or adjusted or they were treated for their UTI, their behavior usually improved, and they were able to return to the long-term care setting.

––––––––––––––

Social workers are one of the largest groups of providers of psychiatric and mental health services in the United States. There is tremendous opportunity for social workers who want to work with the geriatric population within the mental health field. Psychiatric social workers can find employment in a wide range of settings, including inpatient psychiatric treatment centers and outpatient mental health clinics. Within these settings, social workers play an important role in helping older adults with mental health disorders and challenges to attain improved mental health and well-being.

CHAPTER NOTES

1. For further reading about deinstitutionalization, see Torrey, E.F. (2010). Documenting the failure of deinstitutionalization. *Psychiatry, 73*(2), 122–124; Fakhoury, W., & Priebe, S. (2007). Deinstitutionalization and reinstitutionalization: Major changes in the provision of mental healthcare. *Psychiatry, 6*(8), 313–316; Scherl, D.J., & Macht, L.B. (1979). Deinstitutionalization in the absence of consensus. *Hospital & Community Psychiatry, 30*(9), 599–604; Feldman, S. (1983). Out of the hospital, onto the streets: The overselling of benevolence. *The Hastings Center Report, 13*(3), 5–7; FRONTLINE (2005, May 10). Deinstitutionalization: A psychiatric "Titanic." (Excerpt drawn from Chapters 1, 3 and the Appendix of *Out of the shadows: Confronting America's mental illness crisis*, by E. Fuller Torrey, 1997, New York: John Wiley & Sons). *FRONTLINE*. Available at https://www.pbs.org/wgbh/pages/frontline/shows/asylums/special/excerpt.html; Steadman, H.J., Mulvey, E.P., Monahan, J., Robbins, P.C., Appelbaum, P.S., Grisso, T., et al. (1988). Violence by people discharged from acute psychiatric inpatient facilities and by others in the same neighborhoods. *Archives of General Psychiatry, 55*(5), 393–401.

CHAPTER 17

Academia, Advocacy, and Public Policy

KEY POINTS

- Social workers' understanding of human behavior and inter-action and their knowledge of community resources make them valuable contributors to the education of social work students.

- Social work promotes social change, social cohesion, and the empowerment and liberation of people.

- Social workers' belief in the empowerment of older adults helps older persons to become advocates for themselves and for the community.

Social Work Opportunities in Academia

As educators, social workers have a variety of skills and experiences to share with students looking to enter into the profession. Although most teaching positions for social workers at the college or university level are found in schools of social work, there are also opportunities to teach in other higher education departments. In addition to my teaching position at the University of South Florida School of Aging Studies, I also taught courses in nursing and other health-related departments. In this section, I share some of the rewards, benefits, and required skills for social work teaching, as well as research gleaned from a lengthy career of teaching at the university level.

My first opportunity to teach was early in my social work career, when I was asked to teach a course at the University of Buffalo. I was hired as an adjunct faculty member in the College of Health Sciences, where I taught a course on healthcare in the United States. The year was 1979, a time of important debates and discussions about our country's healthcare policies. There was plenty of material that was relevant to the class, particularly Senator Ted Kennedy's historical proposal for universal healthcare coverage. This was the beginning of a passion for teaching that would endure for over 30 years.

Around this time, I also developed an interest in research and writing. Shortly after my first social work job ended with the termination of the Relocation Trauma Counseling Program in Buffalo, I began to analyze program data with the help of the statistician from the Erie County Office for the Aging. I presented several papers on the results of the program, and in 1980, I published my first research article, "Relocation Trauma Counseling for the Elderly: A Demonstration Project" in the *Journal of Gerontological Social Work*.[1]

Throughout my social work career, I continued to teach courses on mental health, aging, and social work, but it wasn't until the publication of my second book that I received an offer to teach full-time. I was working as the director of a nursing home dementia program when I was offered the position of instructor and director of the internship program at University of South Florida's School of Aging Studies. Thus began another chapter in my social work career—one that would last for 13 years.

Because I was the first director of the internship program, I was able to develop the program and my role. The many years that I had worked in the community, my knowledge of community resources, and the professional relationships that I had built in the field were valuable assets in developing placements for my student interns. My social work skills were also important tools in building a bridge between the university and the community. When I retired from the university 13 years later, the internship program was an important component of the University of South Florida School of Aging Studies. I no longer had to call in my favors to get community agencies and facilities to take my interns—now, they were calling me at the beginning of every semester to request an intern.

Beyond pragmatic expertise, there are several characteristics that social work departments look for in hiring faculty. Ideal candidates for teaching should do the following:

- Continue to be good learners by participating in a variety of professional development activities, sharing ideas with their colleagues, and reflecting on classroom interactions and student achievements.

- Know how to modify their teaching strategies according to the student, subject matter, and the learning environment.

- Be concerned with developing their students' critical-thinking skills, problem-solving skills, and problem-solving behaviors.

- Draw on their knowledge of their subject, their knowledge of their learners, and their general pedagogical knowledge to transform the concepts of the discipline into terms that are understandable to students.

- Show interest in their students' personal growth, encourage their independence, and sustain high expectations of them.[2]

Most academic settings require faculty to engage in scholarship. At large universities, this involves an emphasis on grants, research, and publications. If social workers are interested in research, they should consider applying to schools that have a recognized graduate-level culture. For those who are more interested in the teaching aspect of academics, community colleges and liberal arts schools that focus on undergraduate teaching might be a better fit. Faculty members are also expected to serve on various department and university committees to help work on the curriculum or other activities. Student development, faculty governance, and the development of new programs are examples of these types of service-oriented activities.

The Council on Social Work Education (CSWE) is recognized as the accrediting organization for academic social work programs in the United States. Most states mandate CSWE accreditation as part of the education requirement for the professional licensing of social workers. To receive CSWE accreditation, social work programs must demonstrate that the curriculum meets core social work competencies and staffing requirements. Accredited programs must include field experience that connects theory and practice. The CSWE accreditation committee meets onsite with social work faculty and evaluates their professional credentials and approaches to professional development, including curriculum development, communities of practice, mentoring, and consultation and supervision. CSWE also promotes ongoing faculty development by offering training, workshops, and education resources.[3]

Service to the community is an important function of faculty in all social work academic programs. The engagement of faculty in community programs and agencies as board members, consultants, and researchers establishes relationships that benefit both the community and the college or university. Involvement in the community also creates new opportunities for student internships and research sites.

Advocacy and Public Policy

Client advocacy is a skill that is essential to the practice of social work. Social workers develop knowledge and understanding of the needs and issues clients face and the programs and services that meet those needs. They also understand the organizational, legislative, regulatory, and cultural contexts in which human services are situated and are committed to a set of social justice values and ethics that respect and give dignity to clients and community stakeholders. Client advocacy is particularly important when working with older adults.

I became a community activist early in my social work career. As an advocate for my geriatric clients, I soon found that to make life better for individuals, it was often necessary to work for changes in services and policies. Next, I discuss some of my personal experiences as an advocate for older adults.

My involvement with the deinstitutionalization of psychiatric patients and the community mental health movement led to my appointment to the Citizen's Board for the Buffalo General Hospital Community Mental Health Center. For the next several years, I participated in the planning and direction of mental health services in the community. During this time, I also became involved in the women's movement, Planned Parenthood, and even a presidential campaign. In addition to these efforts, my passion for advocacy was especially focused on the care of older adults.

My work with older adults and my personal experiences with family members with dementia made me aware of the lack of quality care and resources available for persons with Alzheimer's and related disorders (ADRD) and their families. I was appointed to the Board of Directors of the Florida Gulf Coast Chapter of the Alzheimer's Association and as the chairperson of the chapter's public policy committee for 10 years. I traveled to Washington, D.C. to meet with legislators to help pass important legislation for Alzheimer's research and care. I was appointed to the Alzheimer's Association National Board Committee on Public Policy and, as a member of a subcommittee on dementia and driving, I worked to develop recommendations for state guidelines on driving restrictions for persons with ADRD. As a member of the Alzheimer's Association's Florida Initiative Public Policy Committee, I was instrumental in the development and passage of legislation that mandated dementia training for staff in nursing homes, assisted living facilities, adult day care, home health services, and hospice. When the legislation passed, making Florida the first state to have dementia-training requirements for all levels of healthcare, I participated in the development of training criteria and certification.[4]

According to the International Association of Schools of Social Work (IASSW) and the International Federation of Social Workers (IFSW), "Social work is a practice-based profession and an academic discipline that promotes social change and development, social cohesion, and the empowerment and liberation of people. Principles of social justice, human rights, collective responsibility, and respect for diversities are central to social work."[5] A social worker's belief in the empowerment of older adults will help older persons to become advocates for themselves and for the community. Because they are the largest percentage of American voters, members of the older generation can help to influence government policies as well.

CHAPTER NOTES

1. Kaplan, M., & Cabral, R.M. (1980). Relocation trauma counseling for the elderly: A demonstration project. *Journal of Gerontological Social Work, 2*(4), 321–329.
2. Ramsden, P., Margetson, D., Martin, E., & Clarke, S. (1995). *Recognizing and rewarding good teaching in Australian higher education.* Canberra: Australian Government Printing Services.
3. Council on Social Work Education (CSWE). (2019). About CSWE accreditation. Retrieved from https://www.cswe.org/Accreditation.aspx
4. Hyer, K., Molinari, V., Kaplan, M., & Jones, S. (2010). Credentialing dementia training: The Florida experience. *International Psychogeriatrics, 22*(6), 864–873.
5. The IFSW General Meeting & the IASSW General Assembly. (2014). Global definition of social work. Retrieved from https://www.ifsw.org/what-is-social-work/global-definition-of-social-work/

The Future of Geriatric Social Work

THE U.S. DEPARTMENT of Labor's Bureau of Labor Statistics reports that the field of social work is growing more than twice as quickly as other fields. Between 2016 and 2020, U.S. jobs are projected to grow by 7%, but careers in social work are expected to increase by an average of 16%.[1] Today's social workers traverse many acute, long-term care, and community-based settings. They are well-positioned to coordinate health and social services for older adults.

Social workers have wonderful opportunities to serve in the highest tradition of their profession by improving the quality of life of older adults. Social work has historically been the leading profession with expertise in navigating complex systems of care. An elder-competent social work labor force will enable older adults and their families to navigate the complex network of health and social services and empower them with the resources and support they need to continue leading productive, satisfying, and independent lives. There is a demand and opportunity for social workers to play an important role in geriatric care like never before. If policymakers want to effectively meet the needs of older adults, they must establish funding and standards for care, taking advantage of the potential for social workers to be key providers. My passion for social work has not abated since retirement. In fact, social work is still in my own future.

It has been over 3 years since I closed the door to my office and ended 41 years of social work practice. At the time, I was grappling with the concept of retirement and beginning to explore my options for the next stage of my life journey. I decided to take some time to figure it out, focusing on travel, family, and writing this book. In the meantime, I explored several possibilities for remaining engaged in the community and in the social work profession. Several options that I considered included working part-time conducting mental capacity evaluations for the courts, continuing my role as a dementia care consultant, and volunteering in community agencies and programs. Nothing seemed to create a spark.

In the summer of 2017, this country experienced multiple natural disasters that affected entire communities in Texas, Florida, and Puerto Rico. Shortly after Hurricane Harvey hit Texas, resulting in massive flooding and the loss of many homes and lives, I received an email from my alma mater. The University at Buffalo School of Social Work sent out an appeal to alumni to volunteer to provide mental health services to storm victims, providing a list of organizations that were mobilizing volunteers. I gave it some thought over the next several days, and it gradually dawned on me that this might be the opportunity to utilize my social work skills that I had been searching for since retirement. I contacted the American Red Cross and began the application process to become a disaster mental health volunteer.

The American Red Cross is widely known as a disaster relief organization, but I was unaware that, in addition to responding to the basic needs of disaster victims, the organization offers mental health services during all disaster relief operations as well as during the recovery phase. The eligibility criteria for disaster mental health volunteers requires them to be licensed as a mental health professional, school psychologist, or psychiatric nurse and to complete extensive training. My application process took several months to complete because the organization had received applications from over 5,000 health and mental health professionals. After passing the background check, I began several hours of training, most of it online. During this time, I was assigned to a local chapter, where I met with the director to discuss my preferences for volunteer assignment. I was surprised to learn that I was the only mental health volunteer in that chapter. After reviewing my professional experience and identifying my interests, it was decided that, in addition to disaster deployment, I would be used as a trainer. I am currently completing the additional training necessary to become a certified trainer and am finding that, after all these years, I am still a social worker.

CHAPTER NOTES

1. Bureau of Labor Statistics, U.S. Department of Labor. (2019). *Occupational outlook handbook, social workers.* Retrieved from https://www.bls.gov/ooh/community-and -social-service/social-workers.htm

Index